ALL ABOUT PRAYER
Basic Aspects to Higher Aspects

Part One

In memory of my dear and godly parents

Late Mr. Albert M. Singh &
Late Mrs. Elizabeth Albert Singh

ALL ABOUT PRAYER

Basic Aspects to Higher Aspects

Part One

Avinash Singh

2013

All About Prayer: Basic Aspects to Higher Aspects - Part One — Published by the Rev. Dr. Ashish Amos of the Indian Society for Promoting Christian Knowledge (ISPCK), Post Box 1585, 1654 Madarsa Road, Kashmere Gate, Delhi-110006.

ISBN : 978-81-8465-330-4

Laser typeset by
ISPCK, Post Box 1585, 1654, Madarsa Road, Kashmere Gate, Delhi-110006.
Tel: 23866322/23
e-mail: *ashish@ispck.org.in* • *ella@ispck.org.in*
website: *www.ispck.org.in*

Dedicated to all

bishops

pastors

evangelists

missionaries

prayer warriors

sunday school teachers

youth leaders

and

all who are passionate about prayer.

Contents

Acknowledgements

There are many people who must be thanked for making this book possible.

I am thankful to God almighty for allowing me to write this book on prayer. It took me one in half years to work on it .

I am thankful for my dear parents (Lt. Mr. Albert M. Singh & Lt. Mrs. Elizabeth. A. Singh) who are now in God's glory. As a family we spent many hours in prayer, and they inspired, motivated, encouraged and supported me to work for the Lord's ministry.

I am also thankful to my former Principals (Rev. Dr.Leaderwell and Rev. Dr. Samson Parekh) of Union Biblical Seminary, Pune where I did my B.D. (Bachelor of Divinity) for their inspiration and encouragement to write a book on prayer. I am really grateful to my present Principal (Rev. Dr. Shekhar Singh) of Union Biblical Seminary, Pune for writing an encouraging comment for my book.

I am very thankful to Respected Bishop Collin. C. Theodore (Moderator Commissary for Lucknow Diocese, Church of North India) for writing a foreword note for my book. Lastly, I am really thankful to all my prayer partners who prayed for me, and for the completion of this book.

May God bless them all

Rev. Avinash Singh

Foreword

I am so happy to know that Rev. Avinash Singh is articulating his thoughts "All About Prayer: From basic Aspects to Higher Aspects – Part One." As we know, prayer is a communication with God and this communication helps to understand the nature of God, and his purpose for his people. I congratulate Rev. Avinash Singh for his very valuable contribution in the form of this book, and I hope the readers will be blessed while reading this spiritual experience. I wish all God's blessings on Rev. Avinash Singh in his pastoral ministry, as a Presbyter in the Diocese of Lucknow, CNI.

With my prayerful blessings,

Bishop Collin C. Theodore,   **Bishop's House**
Moderator's Episcopal Commissary,   25 Mahatma Gandhi Marg
Diocese of Lucknow, CNI   Allahabad-211001, U.P.

Preface

My dear readers, someone made the statement, "When man works, man works; when man prays, God works." I am thankful to my heavenly father who has enabled me to write this book on prayer. God is seeking for people who can pray. Pray is fundamental in the Kingdom of God. It is neither an "extra option" nor a last resort when all other methods fail. Prayerlessness is a sin (1 Samuel 12.23).

God 's plan for the world cannot be accomplished without prayer. It is true that our knowledge about prayer is limited. This book contains many familiar topics and some, which are not discussed or mentioned in many other books written on prayer.

Billy Graham once said: "John Knox prayed, and the results caused Queen Mary to say that she feared the prayer of John Knox more than she feared all the armies of Scotland. John Wesley prayed and revival came to England, sparing the nation the horrors of the French Revolution. Jonathan Edwards prayed, and revival spread throughout the colonies. History has changed time after time because of prayer. I tell you, history could be altered and changed again if people went on their knees in believing prayer. Today we can harness the power of the atom, but very few of us have learned how to develop fully the power of prayers."

I must confess to my readers that I never planned to write a book. I have been completely inspired by my God and Savior, Jesus Christ to do so. This is the revised version of my first book titled, "All about prayer- Basic Aspects to Higher Aspects" which was printed and published by ISPCK.

This time I have divided this book in two parts. The first part deals with the Basics Aspects of prayer, and the Second part deals with the Higher Aspects of prayer.

I am presenting to you the first part of this book "ALL ABOUT PRAYER-Basic Aspects to Higher Aspects of prayer- Part one".

If you would like to be a part of this prayer revolution, here are some ways:

- Be a person of prayer in your church, state or country.

- Gift this book to your friends, family members and relatives to learn about the importance of prayer.

- Feel free to share your comments on my e-mail address (*avinashsinghforjesus@gmail.com*) or write to me at my permanent postal address (Old H. No.23, New No.22, Singh Villa, Yellow Church Campus, Sipri Bazar, Jhansi (U.P.) - 284003, INDIA).

MAY GOD BLESS YOU

Rev. Avinash Singh

Introduction

It gives me great joy to write few words of appreciation and recommendation for the book written by Rev. Avinash Singh. This is an excellent, and yet simple book on prayer. It gives deeper insight about prayer, which is a very vital and important part of Christian life.

Our Lord Jesus Christ while on earth not only encouraged people to pray to the Father, but also spent immense amount of time praying for his disciples, for the world, and for himself - so that he could complete the mission for which he came into the world successfully.

Our Lord Jesus Christ taught people how to pray. The disciples were struggling to pray, and they wanted to know how to pray to the Father. Jesus taught a very simple, but powerful prayer to his disciples, which has become an example to all the Christians around the world. It teaches us how to depend upon God who is our father, creator, sustainer and redeemer. It teaches us the basics of forgiveness, loving one another and our growing relationship with God.

Prayer has the power to multiply. When our Lord Jesus Christ prayed and gave thanks over the five loaves of bread and two fish the food was sufficient for more than five thousand people. It was impossible for the disciples to conceive, but when Jesus prayed over the limited resources it became sufficient for all the people present. Whatever is impossible becomes possible in the sight of God.

Prayer brings healing to the suffering people. James in his letter to the believers reminded them of the importance of prayer. Prayer brings holistic healing in one's total personality.

Prayer is a direct communication with God. We as human beings long for a relationship with God to enhance our spiritual life. The only one way we can improve our relationship with God, is to come into a direct relationship with God, in prayer. We can share all our burdens and sorrows with him because he is willing to listen to us, and help us to resolve our conflicts in life.

I want to congratulate Rev. Avinash Singh for authoring this book which will be very beneficial for believers who want to know 'what is prayer'. What does the word of God say about prayer. and how one can draw closer to God in prayer.

It is my prayer that many will be blessed through this book.

Rev. Dr. Shekhar Singh
Principal
Union Biblical Seminary
Post Box 1425, Bibvewadi,
Pune-411037

Testimony of
Rev. Avinash Singh

I am Rev. Avinash Singh, from Jhansi (U.P.) North India. I am a communicant member of the Sipri Church(yellow church), C.N.I. Jhansi (U.P.). I belong to a staunch Christian family. We are a family of four members including me, my parents, my elder sister. My parents are in God's glory and my elder sister is married. I am in the pastoral ministry and praying and seeking for a life partner.

How I received Jesus Christ as my personal Saviour

As I was born in a Christian family Sunday school was my pivot. Every Sunday, before breakfast, my parents sent me to clean my church with the churchpeon. While cleaning the church I used to think I was close to God, but in reality I was very far. I think, to know God was something familiar to me because I regularly attended all church meetings. As I attended the meetings and cleaned the church I felt I was very famous in my church because everyone understood that I was doing it for God's glory. At that time, my personal motive was to go for the meetings and to do good work believing it was enough to please God. Although I used to clean the church since my childhood I was not keen to know HIM. Whenever I was asked if I had got salvation I would escape answering the question. Actually I was not aware of what salvation meant.

One day I met a servant of God. I had the privilege to talk to him personally. As our conversation began he asked me, "have you received salvation"? Then he asked what do I understood by salvation? I told him it was through my acts of service to the church.

As the Bible says, *"Trust in the Lord with all your heart and lean not on your own understanding"* (Proverbs 3.5).

Soon he came to know that I had not been saved and opened his Bible and read few verses of which one verse Is. 64.6 really talked to me personally. *"All of us have become like one who is unclean; and all our righteous acts are like filthy rags; we all shrivel up like a leaf, and like the wind our sins sweep us away"*.

God gave me the realization that all my religious acts and good works were like filthy rags. That moment I went on my knees and I confessed all my sins, and I realized that I needed a saviour who gives eternal life in Lord Jesus Christ.

As the Bible says, *"For all have sinned and fall short of the glory of Lord."* (Romans 3.23)

"For the wages of sin is death, but the gift of God is eternal life in Christ Jesus our God."(Romans 6.23)

"That if you confess with your mouth,'Jesus is Lord,'and believe in your heart that God raised him from the dead, you will be saved. For it is with your heart that you believe and are justified, and it is with your mouth that you confess and are saved." (Romans 10.9,10)

"Yet to all who received him, to those who believed in his name, he gave the right to become children of God" (John 1.12).

Now, He is my God , and He is my best friend with whom I share everything.

God gave me a heart to invite Him into my life, to accept Him as Lord Jesus Christ, on 4th April 1996.

On that day He taught me through His word, in order to serve the Lord first of all I need to love God, as Lord Jesus said, *"Love the Lord your God with all your heart, and with all your soul, and with all your mind, and with all your strength"* (Mark 12.30).

Earlier, I was not interested in God, and though I obeyed my parent's commands. I never thought that one day I would encounter God in such a manner. I praise God for His merciful act towards me and also for making me His representative.

My testimony is, that after receiving Christ, my Saviour helped me to organize various programmes for the youth, children, Christian leaders along with Bible studies, prayer groups and visits to orphanages in my city and other cities.

I experienced the hand of God, as it was only God's grace that helped me to work to spread His word.

I am really thankful to my Saviour and His faithfulness to His people.

I am grateful to God for His plan for my life. I joined Union Biblical eminary, Pune in 2003 for theological studies (Bachelors of Divinity course). It was God's plan to teach and mould me in such a manner that I would become a useful instrument for the extension of His kingdom, and bring glory to His name. At present I am engaged in Pastoral ministry with the Church of North India, in the Lucknow Diocese.

1

Is Prayer a Gift from God
to Some Believers or for Everyone
who Trusts in Him?

Before we look to the basic aspects of prayer it is important for us to know that prayer is a gift for some believers, or it is for everyone who trusts in the name of Lord and Savior Jesus Christ.

As a member of a family one has all the rights to talk to other family members, discuss with them, know more about them, and share all sorrows and happiness.

The Bible very clearly states,

"For everyone who asks receives; the one who seeks finds; and to the one who knocks, the door will be opened." (Matthew 7:8)

The privilege of prayer is our spiritual right, and we, as Christians have to utilize this right. Prayer shows our relationship with God. Imagine, you are in the family but you are not talking or speaking to each other. This can have various reasons - it could be that you do not have a good relationship with your family; or, that you are not interested in them; or, you have some other problems.

I very firmly believe that prayer is not a gift of God for some believers, but it is for everyone who trusts in Him and wants to talk to the Heavenly Father- at anytime, any place and in any situation.

There is a story about a man, whose daughter asked the local pastor to come and pray with her father. When the Pastor arrived, he found the man lying in bed with his head propped up on two pillows and an empty chair beside his bed. The pastor assumed that the old fellow had been informed of his visit. "I guess you were expecting me," he said. "No, who are you?" "I'm the new pastor of your local church," the pastor replied. "When I saw the empty chair, I figured out you knew I was going to visit you." "Oh yes, the chair," said the bedridden man. "Would you mind closing the door?" Puzzled, the pastor shut the door. "I've never told anyone this, not even my daughter," said the man. "But all of my life I have never known how to pray. At Church I used to hear the pastor talk about prayer, but it always went right over my head. I abandoned any attempt to prayer," the old man continued, until one day about four years ago my best friend said to me, 'Joe, prayer is just a simple matter of having a conversation with Jesus. Here's what I suggest. Sit down on a chair; place an empty chair in front of you, and in faith see Jesus on the chair. It's not spooky because He has promised, "I'll be with you always." You just speak to him and listen to him in the same way you are doing with me right now.'"

"So I tried it and I liked it so much that I do it a couple of hours every day. I'm careful, though. If my daughter saw me talking to an empty chair, she'd either have a nervous breakdown or send me off to the funny farm." The pastor was deeply moved by the story and encouraged the old man to continue on the journey. Then he prayed with him, and returned to the church.

Two nights later the daughter called to tell the pastor that her daddy had died that afternoon. "Did he seem to die in peace?" he asked. "Yes, when I left the house around two' a clock he called me over to his beside, told me one of his corny jokes, and kissed me on the cheek. When I got back from the store an hour later, I found him dead. But there was something strange, In fact, beyond strange-kind of weird. Apparently, just before Daddy died, he leaned over and rested his head on a chair beside the bed."

Sometimes I wonder why God gave us the right to be His children. One of the major reasons is that children always expect their parents to provide the answers to their questions, provide the things which they need, provide the love and care that they require because for the children, apart from their parents, they have no one. Children do not accept strangers; in fact they may even fear strangers. A parent however does not usually bring fear and a child is comfortable to share his/her needs with the parents. God will always bring peace and comfort to His children. While there is a type of fear there... it is a holy fear and a reverence for our Lord.

Prayer is not a gift, it is a privilege, for everyone who is in God. It is a God given facility to approach Him at any moment.

Thought   :   Our relationship with God is shown only through PRAYER.

NOTES

2

What Is Prayer?

Did you know that much of our failure in prayer is because we have not looked into this question, "What is prayer?"

According to Wikipedia, "Prayer is the act of attempt to communicate, commonly with a sequence of words, with a deity or spirit for the purpose of worshipping, requesting guidance, requesting assistance, confessing sins or to express one's thoughts and emotions. The words of prayer may take the form of a hymn, incantation or a spontaneous utterance in the person's praying words. Secularly, the term can also be used as an alternative to "hope"[1] another definition of prayer: "Prayer is the practice of the presence of God. It is the place where pride is abandoned, hope is lifted, and supplication is made."[2] Prayer is basically talking with God. It is simply expressing your heart and spending time with Him.[3] Prayer is not delivering our personal shopping list of

---

[1] *http://en.wikiPedia.org/wiki/Pmyer* (24 January 2008).

[2] *http://www.carm.org/prayer/prayer.htm* (24 January 2008).

[3] *http://psalm121.ca/whatpray.html*

needs[4] Prayer is fellowshipping with the Father- a vital, personal contact with the God who is more than enough.[5] Prayer is the foundation of our relationship with God.[6] Prayer is a work of faith.[7]

In the Bible prayer is defined in various ways: For example,

1. **Prayer is not a vain repetition:** "And when you pray, do not keep on babbling like pagans, for they think they will be heard because of their many words." (Matthew 6:7)

2. **Prayer is to be persistent until we get answers:** "So I say to you: Ask and it will be given to you; seek and you will find; knock and the door will be opened to you. For everyone who asks receives; the one who seeks finds; and to the one who knocks, the door will be opened." (Luke 11.9,10)

3. **Prayer is to be answered according to God's will:** "This is the confidence we have in approaching God: that if we ask anything according to his will, he hears us." (1 John 5.14)

4. **Prayer is not to gratify our material desires:** "When you ask, you do not receive, because you ask with wrong motives, that you may spend what you get on your pleasures. You adulterous people, don't you know that friendship with the world means enmity against God? Therefore, anyone who chooses to be a friend of the world becomes an enemy of God." (James 4.3,4)

---

[4] Debroach Wiley, Ears to hear. (Chennai: YWAM Publishing House, 1982) p. 30.

[5] Carolyn East, Prayers That Avail Much. (New Delhi: National Prayer forum, 2003) p.9.

[6] P.K.D. Lee, Add to your faith.....Excellence (India: Haggai Institute) p.71

[7] Wesley L. Duewel, Mighty Prevailing Power (U.S.A. Zondervan Publishing House, 1990) p. 91.

5. **Prayer is a beseeching to the Lord:** "But Moses sought the favor of the Lord his God. 'Lord,' he said, 'why should your anger burn against your people, whom you brought out of Egypt with great power and a mighty hand?'" (Exodus 32:11)

6. **Prayer is seeking unto God and making a supplication:** "But if you will seek God earnestly and plead with the Almighty," (Job 8:5)

7. **Prayer is drawing near to God:** "But as for me, it is good to be near God. I have made the Sovereign Lord my refuge; I will tell of all your deeds." (Psalm 73:28)

I once read a book that described an incident where Mr. Moody was once addressing a crowd of children in Edinburgh. In order to get their attention he began with a question, " What is prayer?" He paused for a moment to get a reply. To his amazement, scores of little hands shot up all over the hall. He asked one lad to answer; and the answer came at once, clear and correct, "Prayer is an offering of our desires to God for things agreeable to His will, in the name of Christ, with confession of our sins and thankful acknowledgement of His mercies."

The question is, what do we mean by prayer? How do we see prayer? What is our logical definition or understanding about prayer? I believe that a majority of the people who pray, believe that prayer is begging, or putting their demands (in prayer) to God. Bernard Shaw once said, "Common people do not pray; they only beg."

Prayer is not a bending of the will of a reluctant God to our will. "We must not conceive prayer as overcoming God's reluctance," says Archbishop Trench, "but as laying hold of His highest willingness." Brother Lawrence once said, "Prayer is nothing else than a sense of God's presence" – and, that "it is just the practice of the presence of God." "Prayer," says an old Jewish mystic, "is the moment when heaven and earth kiss each other."

God spoke to me through the Book of Psalms with a definition of prayer

> "Trust in him at all times, you people;
> pour out your hearts to him,
> for God is our refuge." (Psalm 62: 8)

In other words I can define prayer as "pouring one's heart to God". Our hearts contain praises, thanksgiving, joy, petitions, anxieties, sorrow, hurts, failure and many other different experiences and emotions, which we cannot share with anybody, but we can share only with God. He is available for all people who believe in Him, and even to those who do not believe in Him, because God is a loving refuge. The Psalmist describes the experience of taking refuge in Him by saying, "The Lord watches over you—

> the LORD IS YOUR SHADE AT YOUR RIGHT HAND;
> the sun will not harm you by day,
> nor the moon by night.." (Psalm 121. 5,6)

In other words we can understand prayer as a "Pouring out the soul before the Lord" (1 Samuel 1: 15). We have to empty ourselves in front of God so He can deal with us according to His will and plan.

Prayer presupposes a belief in the personality of God, his ability and willingness to communicate with us, his personal control of all things, and of all his creatures and all their actions. Prayer is our direct link with heaven. Prayer is a communication process that allows us to talk to God. Praying is like talking to your best friend. It is easy to talk to someone who is willing to listen to you, and who loves you unconditionally.

One of the greatest joys of prayer is securing wonderful answers that seem so long delayed and humanly impossible. James 4:8 says, "Come near to God and he will come near to you. Wash your hands, you sinners, and purify your hearts, you double-minded."

Thought : You will know with confidence that God can hear you when you pray, so open that line of communication. Pray, knowing that no matter how far you roam, your connection with Him can never be lost!

NOTES

3

Prayers in the Old and New Testaments

Dear readers, I will try to point out from the Bible how important it is for us to be passionate about prayer – the whole Bible is filled with prayers.

PRAYERS IN THE OLD TESTAMENT

Genesis

Adam and Eve's talk with God: Genesis 3:8-19

Cain's prayer for mercy; Genesis 4:13-15

Abraham's prayer for a son and for land, the covenant mentioned: Genesis 15:1-18

The covenant of circumcision, Abraham's prayer for Ishmael: Genesis 17:1-26

Abraham pleads for Sodom: Genesis 18:20-33

Abraham's prayer for Abimelech: Genesis 20:17

Abraham's servant's prayer for success and guidance: Genesis 24: 17-19

Isaac's prayer for his barren wife: Genesis 25:21

Rebecca'a prayer for understanding by Rebecca: Genesis 25:22-25

God talks to Jacob: Genesis 28:10-15

Jacob's prayer for deliverance from Esau: Genesis 32:9-12

Exodus

The Israelites' prayer for deliverance:; Exodus 2:23-25; 3:7

Moses' prayer for Pharaoh: Exodus 8:9-15

Moses' prayer for good water: Exodus 15:22-25

Moses' prayer for Israel: Exodus 32:30-35

God speaks to Moses over 100 times in Exodus

Leviticus

God speaks to Moses and Aaron in every chapter of Leviticus

Numbers

The priestly blessing: Numbers 6:22-27

Moses' prayer to God for help, for meat, he wants to die: Numbers 11:10-23

Moses' prayer for Miriam: Numbers 12:1-14

Moses' prayer for a successor: Numbers 27:15-22

God speaks to Moses in most chapters of Numbers

Deuteronomy

Moses' prayer that he may see the Promised Land: Deuteronomy 3:23-24; 34:1-4

The Shema, the most used prayer by the Jews, Jesus called it the most important commandment: Deuteronomy 6:4-9

Joshua and Judges

God offered Joshua prosperity and success, the Formula of Prosperity in the Bible: Joshua 1:6-9

God offered Joshua Jericho: Joshua 6:1-11

Joshua prayed for help: Joshua 7:6-13

Joshua spoke to God in Gideon and the sun stood still: Joshua 10:12-14

The people in Judges listened to God but disobeyed: Judges 2:1-3

Gideon askeds for proof of his call: Judges 6:36-40

Manoah, Samson's father, prayed for guidance: Judges 13:8-14

Samson prayed for water: Judges 15:18-19

Samson prayed for strength: Judges 16:28-30

Ezra

Jews fasted and prayed for a safe journey: Ezra 8: 21, 23

Ezra prayed for the sins of the people: Ezra 9: 5-15

Nehemiah

Nehemiah prayed for the Jews in disgrace: Nehemiah: 1: 3-11

The Israelites prayer of Confession: Nehemiah: 9: 5-38

Esther

Fasting and prayer of the Jews in trouble: Esther 4:3, 15-16

Mordecai's prayer against ruin: Esther 4:1,13, 14

Esther's prayer in fear, for help: Esther 4:16

Job

Job's prayer of fidelity to God: Job 1:20

Job wished death before birth: Job 10:1-3

Psalms of Faith and Life

The best known Psalm and Sacramental Psalms: 23 and, 18, 27, 46, 131, 133.

Psalms of the Church

The Seven Psalms of Zion of the Church: 46, 48, 76, 87, 132, 133, and 134.

Penitential Psalms

"Miserere me, Domine", "have mercy on me, Lord" ... the classic one, used by some religious orders to flagellate themselves: Psalm: 51

Psalm of Wisdom, of the Law of God, the two ways, of Maskil ("of Instruction") The longest Psalm and the longest chapter in the Bible with 176 verse ... the Law of God ... God's word is "a lamp to my feet and a light to my path." (119: 105) : Psalm: 119

Psalms of Lamentation and Petition

Enemies

Psalms: 3, 5, 7, 12, 13, 14, 27, 28, 35, 53, 54, 56, 58, 59, 64, 69, 70, 71, 73, 102, 109, 140, 143.

Imprecatory Psalms

Curses against the enemy or imprecatory Psalms: 5, 6, 11, 12, 35, 37, 40, 52, 54, 56, 58, 69, 79, 83, 109, 137, 139, 143.

Psalms in time of Trouble

Psalms: 61, 86, 141, 143

Collective Lamentations and Petitions

Psalms: 44, 60, 74, 79, 80, 83, 85, 106

Divine Healing Psalms

Psalms: 6, 30, 41, 91, 103,105, 143, 146, 147

At the time of Sickness

Psalms: 6, 30, 31, 38, 39, 41, 71, 88

I have mentioned some, and not all Old Testament prayers so you can have an idea of how much the Bible reveals about the ministry of prayer.

THE NEW TESTAMENT

The Lord's Prayer

The prayer our Lord Jesus taught his disciples, when they asked him "teach us to pray" in the Sermon of the Mount is the most important prayer in the Bible (Mathew 6:9-13).

This is how you should pray,

> "Our Father in heaven,
> hallowed be your name,
> your kingdom come,
> your will be done,
> on earth as it is in heaven.
> Give us today our daily bread.
> And forgive us our debts,
> as we also have forgiven our debtors.
> And lead us not into temptation,
> but deliver us from the evil one.

And, (Luke 11: 1-4) "Our Father, hallowed be Your name, Your kingdom come." Give us each day our daily bread. Forgive us our sins, for we also forgive everyone who sins against us. And lead us not into temptation."

Priestly Prayer

Jesus prayed for Himself

After Jesus looked toward heaven and prayed: "Father, the time has come to glorify your Son, that your Son may glorify you. For you granted him authority over all people that he might give eternal life to all those you have given him. Now this is eternal life: that they may know you, the only true God, and Jesus Christ, whom you have sent. I have brought you glory on earth by completing the work you gave me to do. And now, Father, glorify me in your presence with the glory I had with you before the world began."

Jesus prayed for His Disciples (John 17:11-26)

"I have revealed you to those whom you gave me out of the world. They were yours; you gave them to me and they have obeyed your word. Now they know that everything you have given me comes from you. For I gave them the words you gave me and they accepted them. They knew with certainty that I came from you, and they believed that you sent me. I pray for them. I am not praying for the world, but for those you have given me, for they are yours. All I have is yours, and all you have is mine. And glory has come to me through them. I will remain in the world no longer, but they are still in the world, and I am coming to you. Holy Father, protect them by the power of your name - the name you gave me - so that they may be one as we are one. While I was with them, I protected them and kept them safe by that name you gave me. None has been lost except the one doomed to destruction so that Scripture would be fulfilled. "I am coming to you now, but I say these things while I am still in the world, so that they may have the full measure of my joy within them. I have given them your word and the world has hated them, for they are not of the world any more than I am of the world. My prayer is not that you take them out of the world but that you protect them from the evil one. They are not of the world, even as I am not of it. Sanctify them by the truth; your word is truth. As you sent me into the world, I have sent them into the world. For them I sanctify myself, that they too may be truly sanctified.

Jesus prayed for all believers

"My prayer is not for them alone. I pray also for those who will believe in me through their message, that all of them may be one, Father, just as you are in me and I am in you. May they also be in us so that the world may believe that you have sent me? I have given them the glory that you gave me, that they may be one as we are one: I in them and you in me. May they be brought to complete unity to let the world know that you sent me and have loved them even as you have loved me? Father, I want those you have given me to be with me where I am, and to see my glory, the glory you have given me because you loved me before the creation of the world. Righteous Father, though the world does not know you, I know you, and they know that you have sent me. I have made you known to them, and will continue to make you known in order that the love you have for me may be in them and that I myself may be in them."

BOOK OF ACTS

Pentecost came after 9 days of prayer

Then they returned to Jerusalem from the hill called the Mount of Olives, a Sabbath day's walk from the city. When they arrived, they went upstairs to the room where they were staying. Those present were Peter, John, James and Andrew; Philip and Thomas, Bartholomew and Matthew; James son of Alpheus and Simon the Zealot, and Judas, son of James. They all joined together constantly in prayer, along with the women and Mary the mother of Jesus, and with his brothers. (Acts 1:12-14) ...

The believers' prayer on their release, Peter and John went back to their own people and reported all that the chief priests and elders had said to them. When they heard this, they raised their voices together in prayer to God. "Sovereign Lord," they said, "You made the heaven and the earth and the sea, and everything in them. You spoke by the Holy Spirit through the mouth of your servant, our father David: Why do the nations rage and the peoples plot in vain? The kings of the earth take their stand and the rulers gather together against the Lord and against his Anointed One.' Indeed Herod and Pontius Pilate met together with the Gentiles and the people of Israel in this city to conspire against your holy servant Jesus, whom you anointed. They did what your power and will had decided beforehand should happen.

Now, Lord, consider their threats and enable your servants to speak your word with great boldness. Stretch out your hand to heal and perform miraculous signs and wonders through the name of your holy servant Jesus." After they prayed, the place where they were meeting was shaken. And they were all filled with the Holy Spirit and spoke the word of God boldly. (Acts 4: 23-31)

Stephen's prayer

While they were stoning him, Stephen prayed, "Lord Jesus, receive my spirit." Then he fell on his knees and cried out, "Lord, do not hold this sin against them." When he had said this, he fell asleep. (Acts 7: 59-60)

Peter prayed for the Resurrection of Dorcas

In Joppa there was a disciple named Tabitha (which, when translated, is Dorcas), who was always doing good and helping the poor. About that time, she became sick and died, and her body was washed and placed in an upper room. Lydda was near Joppa; so when the disciples heard that Peter was in Lydda, they sent two men to him and urged him, "Please come at once!" Peter went with them, and when he arrived, he was taken upstairs to the room. All the widows stood around him, crying and showing him the robes and other clothing that Dorcas had made while she was still with them. Peter sent them all out of the room; then he got down on his knees and prayed. Turning toward the dead woman, he said, "Tabitha, get up." She opened her eyes, and seeing Peter she sat up. He took her by the hand and helped her to her feet. Then he called the believers and the widows and presented her to them alive. This became known all over Joppa, and many people believed in the Lord. Peter stayed in Joppa for some time with a tanner named Simon. (Acts 9: 36-40)

Prayer of Cornelius and Peter for enlightenment

Cornelius' call for Peter

At Caesarea there was a man named Cornelius, a centurion in what was known as the Italian Regiment. He and all his family were devout and God-fearing; he gave generously to those in need and prayed to God regularly. One day at about three in the afternoon, he had a vision. He distinctly saw an angel of God, who came to him and said, "Cornelius!" Cornelius stared at him in fear. "What is it, Lord?" he asked. The angel answered, "Your prayers and gifts to the poor have come up as a memorial offering before God. Now send men to Joppa to bring back a man named Simon who is called Peter. He is staying with Simon the tanner, whose house is by the sea." When the angel who spoke to him had gone, Cornelius called two of his servants and a devout soldier who was one of his attendants. He told them everything that had happened and sent them to Joppa. (Acts 10: 1-8)

Peter's Vision

About noon the following day as they were on their journey and approaching the city, Peter went up on the roof to pray. He became hungry and wanted something to eat, and while the meal was being prepared, he fell into a trance. He saw heaven opened and something like a large sheet being let down to earth by its four corners. It contained all kinds of four-footed animals, as well as reptiles of the earth and birds of the air. Then a voice told him, "Get up, Peter. Kill and eat." "Surely not, Lord!" Peter replied. "I have never eaten anything impure or unclean." The voice spoke to him a second time, "Do not call anything impure that God has made clean." This happened three times, and immediately the sheet was taken back to heaven. While Peter was wondering about the meaning of the vision, the men sent by Cornelius found out where

Simon's house was and stopped at the gate. They called out, asking if Simon who was known as Peter was staying there. While Peter was still thinking about the vision, the Spirit said to him, "Simon, three men are looking for you. So get up and go downstairs. Do not hesitate to go with them, for I have sent them." Peter went down and said to the men, ''I'm the one you're looking for. Why have you come?" The men replied, "We have come from Cornelius the centurion. He is a righteous and God-fearing man, who is respected by all the Jewish people. A holy angel told him to have you come to his house so that he could hear what you have to say." Then Peter invited the men into the house to be his guests. (Acts 10: 9-23)

Peter at Cornelius' house

The next day Peter started out with them, and some of the brothers from Joppa went along. The following day he arrived in Caesarea. Cornelius was expecting them and had called together his relatives and close friends. As Peter entered the house; Cornelius met him and fell at his feet in reverence. But Peter made him get up. "Stand up," he said, "I am only a man myself." Talking with him, Peter went inside and found a large gathering of people. He said to them:

"You are well aware that it is against our law for a Jew to associate with a Gentile or visit him. But God has shown me that I should not call any man impure or unclean. So when I was sent for, I came without raising any objection. May I ask why you sent for me?" Cornelius answered: "Four days ago I was in my house praying at this hour, at three in the afternoon. Suddenly a man in shining clothes stood before me and said, Cornelius, God has heard your prayer and remembered your gifts to the poor. Send to Joppa for Simon who is called Peter. He is a guest in the home of Simon the tanner, who lives by the sea.' So I sent for you immediately, and it was good of you to come. Now we are all here in the presence of God to listen to everything the Lord has commanded you to tell us." Then Peter began to speak: "I now realize how true it is that God does not show favoritism but accepts men from every nation who fear him and do what is right. You know the message God sent to the people of Israel, telling the good news of peace through Jesus Christ, who is Lord of all. You know what has happened throughout Judea, beginning in Galilee after the baptism that John preached how God anointed Jesus of Nazareth with the Holy Spirit and power, and how he went around doing good and healing all who were under the power of the devil, because God was with him. We are witnesses of everything he did in the country of the Jews and in Jerusalem. They killed him by hanging him on a tree, bur God raised him from the dead on the third day and caused him to be seen. He was not seen by all the people, but by witnesses whom God had already chosen—by us who ate and drank with him after he rose from the dead. He commanded us to preach to the people and to testify that he is the one whom God appointed as judge of the living and the dead. All the prophets testify about him that everyone who believes in him receives forgiveness of sins through his name." While Peter was still speaking these words, the Holy Spirit came on all who heard the message. The circumcised believers who had come with Peter were astonished that the gift of the Holy Spirit had been poured out even on the Gentiles, for they heard them speaking in tongues and praising God. Then Peter said, "Can anyone keep these people from being baptized with water? They have received the Holy Spirit just as we have." So he ordered that they be baptized in the name of Jesus Christ. Then they asked Peter to stay with them for a few days. (Acts 10:1-47)

Prayers of Christians for Peter

So Peter was kept in prison, but the church was earnestly praying to God for him. The night before Herod was to bring him to trial, Peter was sleeping between two soldiers, bound with two chains, and sentries stood guard at the entrance. Suddenly an angel of the Lord appeared and a light shone in the cell. He struck Peter on the side and woke him up. "Quick, get up!" he said, and the chains fell off Peter's wrists. Then the angel said to him, "Put on your clothes and sandals." And Peter did so. "Wrap your cloak around you and follow me," the angel told him. Peter followed him out of the prison, but he had no idea that what the angel was doing was really happening; he thought he was seeing a vision. They passed the first and second guards and came to the Iron Gate leading to the city. It opened for them by itself, and they went through it. When they had walked the length of one street, suddenly the angel left him. Then Peter came to' himself and said, "Now I know without a doubt that the Lord sent his angel and rescued me from Herod's clutches and from everything the Jewish people were anticipating." When this had dawned on him, he went to the house of Mary the mother of John, also called Mark, where many people had gathered and were praying. Peter knocked at the outer entrance and a servant girl named Rhoda came to answer the door. When she recognized Peter's voice, she was so overjoyed she ran back without opening it and exclaimed, "Peter is at the door!" "You're out of your mind," they told her. When she kept insisting that it was so, they said, "It must be his angel."

But Peter kept on knocking, and when they opened the door and saw him, they were astonished. Peter motioned with his hand for them to be quiet and described how the Lord had brought him out of prison. "Tell James and the brothers about this," he said, and then he left for another place. In the morning, there was no small commotion among the soldiers as to what had become of Peter. After Herod had a thorough search made for him and did not find him, he cross-examined the guards and ordered that they be executed. (Acts 12:5-19)

Paul prayed for the father of Publius

There was an estate nearby that belonged to Publius, the chief official of the island. He welcomed us to his home and for three days entertained us hospitably. His father was sick in bed, suffering from fever and dysentery. Paul went in to see him and, after prayer, placed his hands on him and healed him. When this had happened, the rest of the sick, on the island, came and were cured. They honored us in many ways and when we were ready to sail, they furnished us with the supplies we needed. (Acts 28:7-10)

Prayers in the Epistles

Romans

Paul prayed for the Romans

To all in Rome who are loved by God and called to be saints: Grace and peace to you from God our Father and from the Lord Jesus Christ. First, I thank my God through Jesus Christ for all of you, because your faith is being reported all over the world. God, whom I serve with my whole heart in preaching the gospel of his Son, is my witness how constantly I remember you in my prayers at all times; and 1 pray that now at last by God's will, the way may be opened for me to come to you.– (Romans 1:7-9)

Prayers and the Holy Spirit

In the same way, the Spirit helps us in our weakness. We do not know what we ought to pray for, but the Spirit himself intercedes for us with groans that words cannot express. And he who searches our hearts knows the mind of the Spirit, because the Spirit intercedes for the saints in accordance with God's will – (Romans 8: 26)

Paul prayed for the salvation of Israel.

Brothers, my heart's desire and prayer to God for the Israelites is that they may be saved. (Romans 10:1)

Paul asked for prayers:

"I urge you, brothers, by our Lord Jesus Christ and by the love of the Spirit, to join me in my struggle by praying to God for me. Pray that I may be rescued from the unbelievers in Judea and that my service in Jerusalem may be acceptable to the saints there, so that by God's will I may come to you with joy, and together with you be refreshed. The God of peace be with you all. Amen." (Romans 15:30-33)

1 Corinthians

Eucharistic prayer of Thanksgiving

The Lord Jesus, on the night he was betrayed, took bread, and when he had given thanks, he broke it and said, "This is my body, which is for you; do this in remembrance of me." In the same way, after supper he took the cup, saying, "This cup is the new covenant in my blood; do this, whenever you drink it, in remembrance of me. For whenever you eat this bread and drink this cup, you proclaim the Lord's death until he comes"- I Corinthians 11:23-26.

Prayer and the Spirit

Therefore I tell you that no one who is speaking by the Spirit of God says, "Jesus be cursed," and no one can say, "Jesus is Lord," except by the Holy Spirit. I Corinthians 12:3

Speaking in tongues ... praying in tongues: ... to another speaking in different kinds of tongues, and to still another, the interpretation of tongues. I Corinthians 12: 10

" ... For anyone who speaks in a tongue does not speak to men but to God. Indeed, no one understands him; he utters mysteries with his spirit. But everyone who prophesies speaks to men for their strengthening, encouragement and comfort. He who speaks in a tongue edifies himself, but he who prophesies edifies the church. I would like everyone of you to speak in tongues, but I would rather have you prophesy. He who prophesies is greater than one who speaks in tongues, unless he interprets, so that the church may be edified"- (I Corinthians 14: 2-5)

"For this reason anyone who speaks in a tongue should pray that he may interpret what he says. For if I pray in a tongue, my spirit prays, but my mind is unfruitful. So what shall I do? I will pray with my spirit, but I will also pray with my mind; I will sing with my spirit, but I will also sing with my mind. If you are praising God with your spirit, how can one who finds himself among those who do not understand say "Amen" to your thanksgiving, since he does not know what you are saying? You may be giving thanks well enough, but the other man is not edified." (I Corinthians 14:13-17).

"I thank God that I speak in tongues more than all of you. However, in the church I would rather speak five intelligible words to instruct others, than ten thousand words in a tongue. Brothers, stop thinking like children. Concerning evil be infants, but in your thinking be adults. In the Law, it is written, "Through men of strange tongues and through the lips of foreigners I will speak to this people, but even then they will not listen to me," says the Lord. Tongues, then, are a sign, not for believers but for unbelievers; prophecy is for believers, not for unbelievers. So if the whole church comes together and everyone speaks in tongues and some who do not understand or some unbelievers come in, will they not say that you are out of your mind. But if an unbeliever or someone who does not understand comes in while everybody is prophesying, he will be convinced by all that he is a sinner and will be judged by all, and the secrets of his heart will be laid bare. So, he will fall down and worship God, exclaiming, "God is really among you!" (1 Corinthians 14: 18-25)

Orderly Worship

"What then shall we say, brothers? When you come together, everyone has a hymn, or a word of instruction, a revelation, a tongue or an interpretation. All of these must be done for the strengthening of the church. If anyone speaks in a tongue, two - or at the most three - should speak, one at a time, and someone must interpret. If there is no interpreter, the speaker should keep quiet in the church and speak to himself and God." (1 Corinthians 14: 26-28).

"Therefore, my brothers, be eager to prophesy, and do not forbid speaking in tongues. But everything should be done in a fitting and orderly way" (1 Corinthians 14:39-40).

2 Corinthians

Corinthians prayers for Paul:

"'Indeed, in our hearts we felt the sentence of death. But this happened that we might not rely on ourselves but on God, who raises the dead. He has delivered us from such a deadly peril, and he, will deliver us. On him we have set our hope that he will continue to deliver us, as you help us by your prayers. Then many will give thanks on our behalf for the gracious favour granted to us in answer to the prayers of many." (2 Corinthians 1:9-11)

Paul prayed for grace, the thorn in the flesh

"To keep me from becoming conceited because of these surpassingly great revelations, there was given me a thorn in my flesh, a messenger of Satan, to torment me. Three times, I pleaded with the Lord to take it away from me. However, he said to me, "My grace is sufficient for you, for my power is made perfect in weakness. Therefore, I will boast all the more gladly about my weaknesses, so that Christ's power may rest on me. That is why, for Christ's sake, I delight in weaknesses, in insults, in hardships, in persecutions, in difficulties. For when I am weak, then I am strong." (2 Corinthians 12:8-10)

Prayer against doing wrong

"Now we pray to God that you will not do anything wrong. Not that people will see that we have stood the test but that you do what is right even though we may seem to have failed" - 2 Corinthians 13:7.

Prayer to Jesus, 'The Father and The Spirit'

May the grace of the Lord Jesus Christ, and the love of God, and the fellowship of the Holy Spirit be with you all. (2 Corinthians 13: 4)

Ephesians

Praise be to God the Father

"Praise be to the God and Father of our Lord Jesus Christ, who has blessed us in the heavenly realms with every spiritual blessing in Christ. For He chose us in Him before the creation of the world to be holy and blameless in His sight. In love He predestined us to be adopted as his sons through Jesus Christ, in accordance with His pleasure and will - to the praise of His glorious grace, which he has freely given us in the One He loves. In him we have redemption through his blood, the forgiveness of sins, in accordance with the riches of God's grace that He lavished on us with all wisdom and understanding. And He made known to us the mystery of His will according to His good pleasure, which He purposed in Christ, to be put into effect when the times will have reached their fulfillment - to bring all things in heaven and on earth together under one head, even Christ." (Ephesians 1: 3-10)

Thanksgiving and prayer of Paul

"For this reason, ever since I heard about your faith in the Lord Jesus and your love for all the saints, I have not stopped giving thanks for you, remembering you in my prayers. I keep asking that the God of our Lord Jesus Christ, the glorious Father, may give of the Spirit of wisdom and revelation, so that you may know him better. I pray also that the eyes of your heart may be enlightened in order that you may know the hope to which he has called you, the riches of his glorious inheritance in the saints, and his incomparably great power for us who believe. That power is like the working of his mighty strength, which he exerted in Christ when he raised him from the dead and seated him at his right hand in the heavenly realms, far above all rule and authority, power and dominion, and every title that can be given, not only in the present age but also in the one to come. And God placed all things under his feet and appointed him to be head over everything for the church, which is His body, the fullness of him who fills everything in every way". (Ephesians 1: 15-22)

Paul's Prayer for the Ephesians

"For this reason I kneel before the Father, from whom His whole family in heaven and on earth derives its name. I pray that out of His glorious riches He may strengthen you with power through His Spirit in your inner being, so that Christ may dwell in your hearts through faith. And I pray that you, being rooted and established in love, may have power, together with all the saints, to grasp how wide and long and high and deep is the love of Christ, and to know this love that surpasses knowledge -that you may be filled to the measure of all the fullness of God. Now to him who is able to do immeasurably more than all we ask or imagine, according to His power that is at work within us, to him be glory in the church and in Christ Jesus throughout all generations, forever and ever! Amen." (Ephesians 3:14-21)

Prayer of thanksgiving:

 Pray always, continually, using the "Formula of Happiness" in the Bible - " always giving thanks to God the Father for everything, in the name of our Lord Jesus Christ." (Ephesians 5:20).

Pray in the Spirit on all occasions

"And pray in the Spirit on all occasions with all kinds of prayers and requests. With this in mind, be alert and always keep on praying for all the saints. Pray also for me, that whenever I open my mouth, words may be given me so that I will fearlessly make known the mystery of the gospel, for which I am an ambassador in chains. Pray that I may declare it fearlessly, as I should." (Ephesians 6:18-19)

Philippians

Prayer for Love

"And this is my prayer: that your love may abound more and more in knowledge and depth of insight, so that you may be able to discern what is best and may be pure and blameless until the day of Christ, filled with the fruit of righteousness that comes through Jesus Christ - to the glory and praise of God." (Philippians 1:9-11).

Colossians

Prayer of Thanks

"We always thank God, the Father of our Lord Jesus Christ, when we pray for you, because we have heard of your faith in Christ Jesus and of the love you have for all the saints- the faith and love that spring from the hope that is stored up for you in heaven and that you have already heard about in the word of truth, the gospel that has come to you." (Colossians 1:3-6)

Devote Yourselves to Prayer ... And Pray for Me

"Devote yourselves to prayer, being watchful and thankful. And pray for us, too, that God may open a door for our message, so that we may proclaim the mystery of Christ, for which I am in chains. Pray that I may proclaim it clearly, as I should." (Colossians 4:2-4)

Prayer for knowledge, wisdom and understanding

"For this reason, since the day we heard about you, we have not stopped praying for you and asking God to fill you with the knowledge of his will through all spiritual wisdom and understanding." (Colossians 1:9)

Epaphras' prayer for Christians

"Epaphras, who is one of you and a servant of Christ Jesus, sends greetings. He is always wrestling in prayer for you, that you may stand firm in all the will of God, mature and fully assured." (Colossians 4:12)

1 Thessalonians

Prayer of Thanksgiving

Pray always, continually, using the "Formula of Happiness" in the Bible. "Be joyful always; pray continually; give thanks in all

circumstances, for this is God's will for you in Christ Jesus."
(1 Thessalonians 5:16-18)

The "formula of happiness" as revealed in the Bible: Be joyful always! ... The way to be joyful is to pray constantly ... And the way to pray constantly is give thanks to God always, in all circumstances, for everything. Pray always - continually.

Prayer for sanctification

"May God himself, the God of peace, sanctify you through and through. May your whole spirit, soul and body be kept blameless at the coming of our Lord Jesus Christ. The one who calls you is faithful and he will do it." (1 Thessalonians 5:23)

2 Thessalonians

To be counted as worthy

"With this in mind, we constantly pray for you, that our God may count you worthy of his calling, and that by his power he may fulfill every good purpose of yours and every act prompted by your faith. We pray this so that the name of our Lord Jesus may be glorified in you, and you in him, according to the grace of our God and the Lord Jesus Christ." (2 Thessalonians 1:11-12)

Pray for us

"Finally, brothers, pray for us that the message of the Lord may spread rapidly and be honored, just as it was with you. And pray that we may be delivered from wicked and evil men, for not everyone has faith". (2 Thessalonians 3:1,2)

1 Timothy

Prayers of Christians for kings and authority

"I urge, then, first of all, that requests, prayers, intercession and thanksgiving be made for everyone- for kings and all those in authority, that we may live peaceful and quiet lives in all godliness and holiness." (1 Timothy 2: 1,2)

2 Timothy

Paul's prayer for his disciples

"I thank God, whom I serve, as my forefathers did, with a dear conscience, as night and day I constantly remember you in my prayers. Recalling your tears, I long to see you, so that I may be filled with joy." (2 Timothy 1:3,4)

Philemon

Prayer of thanksgiving

"I always thank my God as I remember you in my prayers, because I hear about your faith in the Lord Jesus and your love for all the saints. I pray that you may be active in sharing your faith, so that you will have a full understanding of every good thing we have in Christ." (Philemon: 4,5)

Hebrews

Prayer for us

"Pray for us. We are sure that we have a clear conscience and desire to live honorably in every way. I particularly urge you to pray so that I may be restored to you soon." (Hebrews 13:18,19)

Prayer to the God of Peace

"May the God of peace, who through the blood of the eternal covenant brought back from the dead our Lord Jesus, that great

Shepherd of the sheep, equip you with everything good for doing his will, and may he work in us what is pleasing to him, through Jesus Christ, to whom be glory for ever and ever. Amen." (Hebrews 13:20,21)

James

The Prayer of Faith

"Is anyone of you in trouble? He should pray. Is anyone happy? Let him sing songs of praise. Is anyone of you sick? He should call the elders of the church to pray over him and anoint him with oil in the name of the Lord. And the prayer offered in faith will make the sick person well; the Lord will raise him up. If he has sinned, he will be forgiven. Therefore confess your sins to each other and pray for each other so that you may be healed. The prayer of a righteous man is powerful and effective." (James 5:13-16)

We should pray for each other as told here in James 5:16 ... and in Romans 15:30; 2 Corinthians 1: 11; Colossians 4:3;1 Thessalonians 5:25; 2 Thessalonians 3:1; Hebrews 13:18.

1 Peter

Praise to God for a Living Hope

"Praise be to God and Father of our Lord Jesus Christ! In his great mercy he has given us new birth into a living hope through the resurrection of Jesus Christ from the dead, and into an inheritance that can never perish, spoil or fade - kept in heaven for you, who through faith are shielded by God's power until the coming of the salvation that is ready to be revealed in the last time. In this you greatly rejoice, though now for a little while you may have had to suffer grief in all kinds of trials. These have come so that your faith - of greater worth than gold, which perishes even though refined by fire - may be proved genuine and may result in praise, glory and honor when Jesus Christ is revealed. Though you have not seen him, you love him; and even though you do not see him now, you believe in him and are filled with an inexpressible and glorious joy, for you are receiving the goal of your faith, the salvation of your souls." (1 Peter 1:3-9)

1 John

Prayer of Petition

"This is the confidence we have in approaching God: that if we ask anything according to his will, he hears us. And if we know that he hears us - whatever we ask - we know that we have what we asked of him." (1 John 5:14,15)

Jude

Pray in the Spirit

"But you, dear friends, build yourselves up in your most holy faith and pray in the Holy Spirit. Keep yourselves in God's love as you wait for the mercy of our Lord Jesus Christ to bring you to eternal life." (Jude 20,21)

Thought   :   There are many other prayers in the Old and New Testaments that are not mentioned here. These prayers given above are just to encourage Christians in their faith in how important prayer is in their lives.

NOTES

4

Different Religious
Attitudes Towards Prayer

I want to confess at this point that I have not done a deep study on the attitude of people from different religions towards prayer. This chapter deals with attitudes of people from different religions towards prayer in a general manner.

Prayer is an active effort to communicate with a deity or spirit, either to offer praise, to make a request, seek guidance, confess sins, or simply to express one's thoughts and emotions.

JEWISH PRAYER

Jews pray three times a day; and more, on special days such as the Sabbath and Jewish holidays. The Siddur is the prayer book used by Jews all over the world, containing a set order of daily prayers. Jewish prayer is usually described as having two aspects: kavanah (intention) and keva (the ritualistic, structured elements).

The most important Jewish prayers are the Shema Yisrael ("Hear O Israel") and the Amidah ("the standing prayer"). The Jews consider the best form of prayer is when people pray together;

for example, ten people (minyan) are required in order to pray in synagogue. They believe that the the stronger the connection is stronger when there are more people.

THE SIKHS

Sikhs believe that a true prayer is a wonderful channel through which the powerful current of love flows from the humble, yearning heart of a Sikh to the Lotus feet of his beloved Satguru. It unites the lover with the beloved Satguru in a true bond of love. A sincere prayer from the heart cannot go unheard, unheeded and un-responded.

A true prayer involves total submission. It is the total surrender at the lotus feet of the Lord. It rises from total humility of the heart; the egoistic 'I' and 'Haumain' remain neutralized. There is no assertion of individuality. A true sense of meekness and emptiness takes over during prayer.

"True bliss is experienced when the ego is non-existent. True bliss fills the void created by the exit of ego, of the total surrender of the ego at the lotus feet of the Lord. With ego surrendered, there is no more seeking, all desires disappear, the sweet will and bliss of the Lord takes over."Guru Granth Sahib[1]

ISLAMIC PRAYER

Prayer (Salah), in the sense of worship, is the second pillar of Islam. Prayer is obligatory and must be performed five times a day. These five times are dawn (Fajr), immediately after noon (Dhuhr), mid-afternoon (Asr), sunset (Maghrib), and early night (Isha). Ritual cleanliness and ablution are required before prayer, as are clean clothes and location, and the removal of shoes. One may pray

---

[1] *http://wwww.istholistic.com/Prayer/hol_sikh-prayer.htm* (24th Jan. 2008)

individually or communally, at home, outside, virtually any clean place, as well as in a mosque, though a mosque is preferred above the others. There is special for prayer on Fridays, at noon, called Jum'ah. It is obligatory and is to be done in a mosque with a congregation. It is accompanied by a sermon (Khutbah), and it replaces the normal Dhuhr prayer.[2]

NEOPAGAN PRAYERS

Many modern Neopagans pray to various gods. The most commonly worshipped gods are those of Pre-Christian Europe, such as Celtic, Norse or Graeco-Roman gods. Prayer can vary from sect to sect, and with some (such as Wicca) prayer may also be associated with ritual magic.

PRAYER IN EASTERN RELIGIONS

In contrast with Western religion, Eastern religion mostly discards worship, and places devotional emphasis on the practice of meditation, along with scriptural study.

BUDDHISM

"It allows us to turn our hearts and minds to the beneficial, rousing our thoughts and actions towards awakening."G.R. Lewis

Buddhist prayer is a practice to awaken ones inherent inner capacities of strength, compassion and wisdom rather than to petition for external forces based on fear, idolizing and worldly or heavenly gain. Buddhist prayer is a form of meditation- it is a form of inner reconditioning. Buddhist prayer replaces the negative with the virtuous and helps us to have the blessings of Life.

---

[2] *http://www.angelfine.com/ak5/ashhad4u/lintroislam/inrtol.htm* (24th Jan. 2008).

The wonderful thing about prayer practice is that it can be done anywhere and at anytime, transforming the ordinary and mundane into the path of awakening. Prayer enriches lives with deep spiritual connection and makes every moment special, manifesting the Pure Land here and now.[3]

There is an example of a popular prayer below, adapted from Shatideva's 8th century Indian prayer.

Metta Karuna Prayer

Oneness of Life and Light,

Entrusting in your Great Compassion,

May you shed the foolishness in me,

Transforming me into a conduit of Love.

May I be a medicine for the sick and weary,

Nursing their afflictions until they are cured;

May I become food and drink,

During time of famine,

May I protect the helpless and the poor,

May I be a lamp,

For those who need your Light,

May I be a bed for those who need rest,

 And guide all seekers to the Other Shore.

May all find happiness through my actions,

 And let no one suffer because of me.

Whether they love or hate me,

Whether they hurt or wrong me,

May they all realize true entrusting,

Through Other Power,

---

[3] *http://buddhistfaith.tripod.com/buddhistprayer/id5.html* (24th Jan. 2008).

And realize Supreme Nirvana.
Namo Amida Buddha.[4]

HINDUISM

Hinduism has incorporated many kinds of prayers (Sanskrit: prarthana), from fire-based rituals to philosophical musings. While chanting involves 'by dictum' recitation of timeless verses, 'dhyanam' involves deep meditation (however short or long) on the preferred deity. While the object to which prayers are offered could be a person (as in Krishna, Shiva) it could also be simple plain, formless meditation as practiced by ancient sages. All of these are directed towards fulfilling personal needs or, deep spiritual enlightenment. Ritual invocation was very much a part of the Vedic religion and these fill their sacred texts. In fact, the most sacred texts of the Hindus, the Vedas, are a large collection of mantras and prayer rituals. Classical Hinduism came to focus on extolling a single supreme force, Brahman, who is manifested in several lower forms as the familiar gods of the Hindu pantheon. Hindus in India have numerous devotional movements. Hindus may pray to the highest absolute God Brahman, or more commonly to his three manifestations namely the creator god called Brahma, the preserver god called Vishnu, and the destroyer god (so that the creation cycle can start afresh) Shiva, At the next level they pray to Vishnu's avatars (earthly appearances) Rama and Krishna. There are also many other male and female deities.

Usually, like most Christians, the Hindus pray by joining their palms together. This hand gesture is similar to the customary, symbolic Indian greeting – 'namaste'. In India, it is the Brahmins who pray, and very few others. Even a millionaire merchant, of any other caste, must get a Brahmin to say his prayers for him.

---

[4] *http://buddhistfaith.tripod.com/pureland_sangha/id4html* (24th Jan. 2008).

Hindus in India have numerous devotional movements. The following prayer is the essence of all Vedic ceremonies, and continues to be invoked even today in Hindu temples all over India and around the world:

Asato Ma Sat Gamaya
Tamaso Ma Jyotir Gamaya
Mrityor Ma Amritam Gamaya
Om Shanti Shanti Shanti.

"Lead us from untruth to truth; Lead us from darkness to light; Lead us from death to immortality; Aum -the universal sound of God- Let there be peace, peace, peace."[5]

PRAYER IN JAINISM

Although Jains believe that no spirit or divine being can assist them on their path, they do hold some influence, and on special occasions, Jains will pray for right knowledge to the twenty-four Tirthankaras (saintly teachers).[6]

The Universal Jain Prayer
Namokar Mantra

Nama Arihantanam	-	I bow to the enlightened beings
Nama Siddhanam	-	I bow to the liberated souls
Nama Ayariyanam	-	I bow to religious leaders
Nama Uvajjayanam	-	I bow to religious teachers
Nama Loe Sawa Sahunam	-	I bow to all ascetics of the world
Eso Panch Namukkaro	-	These five salutations are capable

---

[5] *http://en.wikipedia.org/wiki/Prayer_in_Hinduism* (24th Jan. 2008).

[6] *http://en.wikipedia.org/wiki/Prayer_in_western_religions* (18th Feb. 2007).

of Savva Pava Panasano   destroying all sins.

Mangalanancha Savvesin

Padhamam Havai Mangalam   And they are the most capable

Pava Panasanoauspicious   of all benedictions.

In this prayer, the Jains salute the virtues of the five benevolent beings. They do not pray to a specific Tirthankar or ascetic by name. By saluting them, the Jains receive inspiration from the five benevolent beings for the right path of true happiness, and total freedom from the miseries of life.[7]

While this is some information which I collected from different religions about prayer, I would be happy if you could share with me any other information on this subject.

---

[7] *http://www.isholistic.com/Prayer/hol_jainism.htm* (24th Jan. 2008).

NOTES

5

What Does Prayer Require?

What does prayer require? I have listed below, some points from the Bible. There are many other important points connected with these main points. Some of them will be helpful for all readers to learn about what prayer requires.

PRAISE

Praise is the first requirement in prayer. In the book of Habakkuk the author emphasises the importance of praise.

Habakkuk 3:17,18

"Though the fig tree does not bud
    and there are no grapes on the vines,
though the olive crop fails
    and the fields produce no food,
though there are no sheep in the pen
    and no cattle in the stalls,
yet I will rejoice in the LORD,
    I will be joyful in God my Saviour."

Hallesby writes, "When I give thanks, my thoughts still circle about myself, but in praise my soul ascends to self-forgetting adoration, seeing and praising only the majesty and power of God, His grace and redemption."[1]

Praise is something that is not dependent on circumstances, but praise is offered to our God the Father in the midst of any situation we undergo. Some people mistakenly believe that we praise God only when our work is completed successfully. It is not the only time to praise God. It is as if we say, "Praise the Lord" on getting something we desire; but, if we do not get what we desire we will not praise Him. That is not what the Lord Jesus expects from His people.

The Psalmist said in the Psalms:
"May the peoples praise you, God;
   may all the peoples praise you.
[6] The land yields its harvest;
   God, our God, blesses us.

[7] May God bless us still,
   so that all the ends of the earth will fear him." - Psalm
   67:5-7

Huegel, an experienced missionary to Mexico, has said that often when prayer does not bring the answer, adding praise will lead to victory. He states, "There is power in praise which prayer does not have. Of course, the distinction between the two is artificial... The highest expression of faith is not prayer in its ordinary sense of petition, but prayer in its sublimest expression of praise."

---

[1] O. Hallesby Pmyer (London: Hodder & Stoughton, 1936), p.207.

Let our praise to God not depend on our will but fully depend on God's will.

THANKSGIVING

The second requirement in prayer is thanksgiving. In the account of the ten lepers, in the Gospel of Luke, after being healed by Jesus, all of them went back except one who came back to Jesus to give him thanks. Jesus asked him where the other nine were? Did they not get healing also? Often we fast or pray for hours because we want God to intervene in a certain situation. When God responds to our prayer, how many times do we thank our Abba Father?

The book of Colossians tells us ...

"And whatever you do, whether in word or deed, do it all in the name of the Lord Jesus, giving thanks to God the Father through him." (Colossians 3:17)

REPENTANCE

The third requirement in prayer is repentance. The Messiah came and preached a message of repentance (Mark 1:15), stressing that all men needed to repent (Luke 13:1-50. Jesus summoned his followers to turn and become like children (Matthew 18:3). Jesus also differed from His predecessors in His proclamation of repentance. He related it closely to the arrival of the kingdom of God (Mark 1:14,15) and specifically associated it with one's acceptance of Him. Those who were unrepentant were those who rejected Him (Luke 10:8-15). Until we become a part of His family, we have no right to ask Him for anything except forgiveness of sins. Think about the orphan children in this world – those who have no parents and have no right to ask others to do anything for them. They accept whatever people give them. If, however, they had parents, they would not only have the right to ask but also have the blessing of all the inheritance promised to them by their parents; and to share their joys and sorrows with their parents. As Christians we belong to the family of Christ and have the right to forgiveness of sins, and to inherit the Kingdom of God. This can be when we accept Jesus as our personal Saviour. " If you declare with your mouth, "Jesus is Lord," and believe in your heart that God raised him from the dead, you will be saved. For it is with your heart that you believe and are justified, and it is with your mouth that you profess your faith and are saved." (Romans 10:9,10)

One promise from God, on condition of repentance is "if my people, who are called by my name, will humble themselves and pray and seek my face and turn from their wicked ways, then I will hear from heaven, and I will forgive their sin and will heal their land." (2 Chronicles 7:14)

INTERCESSION

The fourth requirement in prayer is intercession. The act of intervening or mediating between different parties; is an act of praying to God particularly on behalf of another person. Most often our prayers pertain only to ourselves, our families, our communities ; and we don't consider praying for others. Paul urged all the believers to pray for everyone. "I urge, then, first of all, that petitions, prayers, intercession and thanksgiving be made for all people—." (1 Timothy 2:1)

Andrew Murray, "Every act of grace in Christ has been preceded by, and owes its power to intercession."[2]

---

[2] Andrew Murray, Ministry of Intercession (New York: Revell, 1898) p.2.

TALKING IN SPIRIT

The fifth requirement in prayer is talking in Spirit. According to Paul, the Spirit is important in the life of believers in order to have a relationship with God. The Spirit is a gracious personal presence who lives in the one who has confessed that Jesus Christ is Lord.

Paul argued with the Galatians that legalism and the way of faith are incompatible. God's Spirit comes to us as a gift based on our faith in Christ and His grace. " You foolish Galatians! Who has bewitched you? Before your very eyes Jesus Christ was clearly portrayed as crucified. I would like to learn just one thing from you: Did you receive the Spirit by the works of the law, or by believing what you heard? Are you so foolish? After beginning by means of the Spirit, are you now trying to finish by means of the flesh? Have you experienced so much in vain—if it really was in vain? So again I ask, does God give you his Spirit and work miracles among you by the works of the law, or by your believing what you heard? So also Abraham "believed God, and it was credited to him as righteousness." (Galatians 3:1-6)

FASTING

The sixth requirement in prayer is fasting. *Unger's Bible Dictionary* explains that the word *fast* in the Bible is from the Hebrew word *sum,* meaning "to cover" the mouth, or from the Greek word *nesteuo,* meaning "to abstain." For spiritual purposes, it means to go without eating and drinking (Esther 4:16).

The Bible gives examples of God's people occasionally combining fasting with their prayers so as to stir up their zeal and renew their dedication and commitment to Him. King David wrote, "I humbled myself with fasting" (Psalm 35:13). Fasting is a means of getting our minds back on the reality that we are not self-sufficient. Fasting helps us realize just how fragile we are and how much we depend on things beyond ourselves.

The Bible records that great men of faith like Moses, Elijah, Daniel, Paul and Jesus Himself fasted so that they might draw closer to God (Exodus 34:28; 1 Kings 19:8; Daniel 9:3; Daniel 10: 2,3 ; 2 Corinthians 11:27; Matthew 4:2). Jesus knew that, once He was no longer there in the flesh with them, His true disciples would, at times, need to fast to regain and renew their zeal to serve Him (Mark 2:18-20).

James tells us, "Draw near to God and He will draw near to you" (James 4:8). Constant prayer and occasional fasting help us to do this.

Different ways of fasting are mentioned in the Bible:

- No food: (Matthew 4:1,2; Luke 4:2)

- No food and no water for three days: (Esther 4:16; Ezra 10: 6;, and Acts 9:9)

- Some food items are eliminated for the period of the fast: (Daniel 1:15,16; 10:2,3)

  The Bible mentions clearly the people of God who fasted and prayed on different occasions, for different reasons:

- Moses spent forty days on Mount Sinai on two occasions, without eating or drinking, mourning over Israel's sin: (Exodus 24: 18, 34: 28; Deuteronomy 9: 9, 18; 10:10)

- Jehoshaphat proclaimed a fast throughout Judah to seek YHWH for fear of the armies of Ammon and Moab: (2 Chronicles 20:3)

- Ezra called a fast to seek God's protection for those leaving Babylon for Israel: (Ezra 8:21-23)

- YHWH called the people to return to Him with fasting, rending their hearts, not their garments; Joel calls for a fast: (Joel 2: 12 – 15)

- Jesus fasted forty days in the wilderness, and was tempted by the devil: (Mathew 4: 2; Luke 4: 2)

- Jesus said that this kind of demon only went out with prayer and fasting: (Mathew 17: 20; Mark 9: 29)

- Paul and Barnabas appointed elders in the churches, with prayers and fasting: (Acts 14:23)

- Paul listed "fasting" as one among the hardships he suffered as a mark of his apostleship: (2 Corinthians 6:5; 11:27

Andrew Bonar defined fasting as abstaining from everything that hindered prayer. The great leaders of the reformation, in their spiritual warfare to restore purity to the Church, maintained the spiritual discipline of fasting. John Wesley preached many sermons on fasting and prayer. He said, "The man who never fasts is no more in the way to heaven than the man who never prays."[3]

TEARS AND LOUD CRIES

The seventh requirement in prayer is tears and loud cries. Think about the people whom you like and consider a good friend on this earth. You share every emotion whether it is joy, tears, love, success or failure with them. This is because you love them and you want them to know everything about you. You are not formal in front of them. Our relationship with God is deeper for we pour our hearts out in front of Him. The expression of our Savior in

---

[3] John Wesley, "Causes of Inefficiency of Christianity," Sermom on Several Occasions, ed. Thomas, Jackson, 2 Vols. (New York: T. Mason and G. Lane, :840), 2:440.

prayer is described in Hebrews 5: 7, "During the days of Jesus' life on earth, he offered up prayers and petitions with fervent cries and tears to the one who could save him from death, and he was heard because of his reverent submission." It is also mentioned in the Gospel of Luke 19:10, "For the Son of Man came to seek and to save what was lost." He shed tears not for Himself, but for the people who were lost and we, as ministers of the gospel are called to do the same.

One should never be ashamed to tears shed in loving intercession. In fact, they testify to God the depth of your relationship with those for whom you intercede, the intensity of longing which underlies your intercession, and serves as a testimony of the Holy Spirit praying through you. Tears add a personal and private dimension of poignancy and power.[4]

World famous Evangelist, Billy Graham stated in one of his books, "Tears shed for self are tears of weakness, but tears shed for others are a sign of strength." Now the question is what should we express when we pray? It's very important. This is not found in the gospel but is mentioned in the epistles. The people who see our Lord Jesus Christ from a distance know what kind of person he was. A passion for the ministry starts in prayer. What is your passion in the ministry of Christ? Is it position, personal benefit, popularity or "PRAYER"?

---

[4] Welsey L. Duewel, Touch the World Through Prayer. (U.S.A.: Zondervan Publishing House), p. 71.

PROCLAIMING PROMISES MENTIONED IN THE BIBLE

The eighth requirement in prayer is to proclaim promises mentioned in the Bible. The Psalmist said to the Lord "Sustain me according to your promise, and I will be ; do not let my hopes be dashed." (Psalm 119:116)

Some verses in the Bible, with promises are:

"If my people, who are called by my name, will humble themselves and pray and seek my face and turn from their wicked ways, then will I hear from heaven, and will forgive their sin and will heal their land." (2 Chronicles 7:14)

"Ask and it will be given to you; seek and you will find; knock and the door will be opened to you. For everyone who asks receives; the one who seeks finds; and to the one who knocks, the door will be opened." (Mathew 7:7,8)

"Ask of me, and I will make the nations your inheritance, the ends of the earth your possession." (Psalm 2:8)

Always remind yourselves of the promises that are available in the Bible for His chosen ones. And All we have to do is to recall them and mention them in our prayers. These promises empower believers, for,

- He made promises to fulfil, not to impress

- He made promises to keep, not to reject

- He made promises to deliver us, not demolish us

- He made promises to regenerate us, not to neglect us.

- He made promises to purify and cleanse us.

PRAYER REQUIRES OUR WHOLE SELVES

The ninth requirement in prayer is our whole selves. In the book *The Essentials of Prayer* by E. M. Bounds, the author sums that up briefly - the entire man, without reservation, must love God. So it takes the same entire man to do the praying which God requires of him . All of the powers of man must be engaged in it. God cannot tolerate a divided heart in the love He requires of men, neither can He bear with a divided man in praying.

In Psalm 119, the Psalmist teaches this very truth in these words:

"Blessed are they that keep his testimonies, and that seek him with the whole heart."

It takes whole-hearted men to keep God's commandments and it demands the same sort of men to seek God. These are the ones who are counted "blessed." It is upon these wholehearted ones that God's approval rests.

Bringing the case closer home to himself the Psalmist makes this declaration as to his practice: "With my whole heart have I sought thee; O let me not wander from thy commandments."

And further on, giving us his prayer for a wise and understanding heart, he tells us his purposes concerning the keeping of God's law:

"Give me understanding and I shall keep thy law; Yea, I shall observe it with my whole heart."

Just as a whole heart is required to be given to God, to gladly and fully obey God's commandments; so also is a whole heart required to for effectual prayer.

Dear Readers, I have mentioned here some requirements for prayer. If there are any others you have identified through your own spiritual experiences of God's word, you can add it to the space below.

NOTES

6

How Some People Define Prayer?

Some definitions about prayer

The major concern of the devil is to keep Christians away from praying. He fears nothing from prayerless studies, prayerless work, and prayerless religion. He laughs at our toil, mocks at our wisdom, but trembles when we pray. - *Samuel Chadwick*

Prayer changes things by changing people. - *Ernest G. Sangster*

The best and sweetest flowers of paradise God gives to His people when they kneel on their knees; prayer is the gateway to heaven - the key to let us into paradise. - *T. S. Brooks*

Prayer is the risen Jesus coming in with His resurrection power, given free rein in our lives, and then using His authority to enter any situation to change things. - *Ole Kristian Hallesby*

Common people do not pray; they only beg. - *Bernard Shaw*

Prayer does not mean asking God for all kinds of things we want; rather it is the desire for God Himself, the only Giver of Life. - *Sadhu Sundar Singh.*

In prayer it is better to have a heart without words than words without a heart. - *John Bunyan*

Prayer needs no speech. - *M. K. Gandhi*

Prayer is the voice of faith. - *Martin Luther*

Prayer is like the dove that Noah sent forth, which blessed him not only when it returned with an olive-leaf in its mouth, but when it never returned at all. - *Robinsons Jobs*

Prayer does not equip us for the Greater work. Prayer is the Greater work. - *Oswald Chambers*

Prayer is the most important work on earth. Intercessors are the most important people on earth. - *Zacharias Tanee Fomum*

The act of praying is the very highest of which human mind is capable; praying, that is, with the total concentration of the faculties. The great mass of worldly men and of learned men are absolutely incapable of prayer. - *Samuel Taylor Coleridge*

Prayer is words of humans and acts of the Divine. - *Avinash Singh*

Sometimes the answer to prayer is not that it changes life, but that it changes you. -James *Dillet Freeman*

Prayer is when you talk to God ; meditation is when you listen to God. - *Diana Robinson*

Prayer will make a man cease from sin, or sin win entice a man to cease from prayer. - *John Bunyan*

Pray often; for prayer is a shield to the soul, a sacrifice to God, and a scourge for Satan. -John Bunyan

Prayer is not asking. It is a longing of a true soul. It is a daily admission of one's weakness. It is better in prayer to have a heart without words than words without a heart. – *John Bunyan*

The most eloquent prayer is the prayer through hands that heal and bless. The highest form of worship is the worship of unselfish Christian service. The greatest form of praise is the sound of consecrated feet seeking out the lost and helpless. - *Billy Graham*

To be a Christian without prayer is no more possible than to be alive without breathing. - *Martin Luther King, Jr*

Prayer enables us to transform the world, because is transforms us. - *Marianne Williamson*

Prayer is as natural an expression of faith as breathing is of life. -*Jonathan Edwards*

Prayer is the voice of faith. - *William Van Horne*

The function of prayer is not to influence God, but rather to change the nature of the one who prays. - *Soren Kierkegaard*

There is nothing in the world drearier than a prayer that attempts to inform God of anything at all. - *Edward N. West*

Prayer is simply a two-way conversation between you and God.- *Billy Graham*

Pray as though everything depended on God. Work as though everything depended on you. - *Saint Augustine*

There are many things that are essential to arriving at true peace of mind, and one of the most important is faith, which cannot be acquired without prayer. - *John Wooden*

http://hannahscupboard.com/prayer-quotes.html

Prayer does not fit us for the greater work; prayer is the greater work. - *Oswald Chambers*

Prayer requires more of the heart than the tongue. - *Adam Clarke*

Effective prayer is prayer that attains what it seeks. It is prayer that moves God, effecting its end. - *Charles Finney*

God does nothing but by prayer, and everything with it. - *John Wesley*

To pray in Jesus' name means to pray in his spirit, in his compassion, in his love, in his outrage, in his concern. In other words, it means to pray a prayer that Jesus himself might pray. - *Kenneth L. Wilson*

http://www.goodreads.com/quotes/tag/prayer

The function of prayer is not to influence God, but rather to change the nature of the one who prays. - *Søren Kierkegaard*

Let us never forget to pray. God lives. He is near. He is real. He is not only aware of us but cares for us. He is our Father. He is accessible to all who will seek Him. - *Gordon B. Hinckley*

Prayer is not asking. Prayer is putting oneself in the hands of God, at His disposition, and listening to His voice in the depth of our hearts. - *Mother Teresa*

The more you pray, the less you'll panic. The more you worship, the less you worry. You'll feel more patient and less pressured. - *Rick Warren*

A prayer couched in the words of the soul, is far more powerful than any ritual. - *Paulo Coelho*

I have so much to do that I shall spend the first three hours in prayer. - *Martin Luther*

Answered prayer is the interchange of love between the Father and His child. - *Andrew Murray*

Prayer is like water - something you can't imagine has the strength or power to do any good, and yet give it time and it can change the lay of the land. - *Jodi Picoult*

Pray the largest prayers. You cannot think a prayer so large that God, in answering it, will not wish you had made it larger. Pray not for crutches but for wings. - *Phillips Brooks*

Prayer is the link between God's inexhaustible resources and people's needs...God is the source of power, but we are the instrument He uses to link the two together. - *Charles F. Stanley*

We have to pray with our eyes on God, not on the difficulties. - *Oswald Chambers*

Praying and sinning will never live together in the same heart. Prayer will consume sin, or sin will choke prayer. - *J.C. Ryle*

Do not have your concert first, and then tune your instrument afterwards. Begin the day with the Word of God and prayer, and first of all get into harmony with Him. - *J. Hudson Taylor*

Thought : These are some definitions of prayer. I urge my readers to make their own definitions of prayer with their personal experiences with God.

NOTES

7

Why Should We Pray?

In August 2005, Newsweek and beliefnet asked 1,400 Americans what they believed in, and how they practised their faith. One of the questions was this: What do you think is the most important purpose of prayer?

HERE ARE THEIR RESPONSES

1. To seek God's guidance (27%).

2. To thank God. (23%)

3. To be close to God or the divine (19%)

4. To help others (13%)

5. To improve a person's life (9%)

6. Other (4%) Don't know (5%)

Have you ever had a close, intimate and satisfying relationship with someone you never talked to? Of course you haven't and it's ridiculous to think it's possible. So why would we pretend to have a close relationship with God, without prayer? 'To be human is to pray ... We are called to be continuously formed and be transformed by the thought of God within us. Prayer is a discipline and a dedication to paying attention. Without the single-minded attentiveness of prayer we will rarely hear anything worth repeating; or, catch a vision worth asking anyone else to gaze upon. ("The Spiritual Life" by John H. Westerhoff III and John D. Eusden (Seabury))

P.K.D. Lee explains the need of a prayer, "Prayer is basically communication and it means consultation with God in all aspects of life, even the insignificant."[1]

The Bible says," The earth is the Lord's and everything in it, the world, and all who live in it;" Psalm 24.1. When everything belongs to God then why worry? You have to talk (pray) to God, who is the creator of everything. In other words, we pray to God, who is the creator of everything, and only He has authority over everything. In the New Testament, the Lord Jesus told his disciples, " ... All authority in heaven and on earth has been given to me." Matthew 28.18.

I have come across many people in my pastoral ministry who have told me that God did not hear them. The question here is, " Why is that so?" A simple answer is, that prayer is a two way street. We talk to God and He talks to us. He speaks to us, revealing Himself to us through prayer. There have been times when I have been puzzled about how something was going to work out in my life. It was through prayer that God calmed my fears and uncertainties by answering my prayers and further building my trust in Him. He helps us recognize all things are possible when we believe in Him. He comforts those who seek Him

---

[1] P.K.D. lee, Add to Your Faith... Excellence. Haggai Institute Publications, (2000), p. 71.

wholeheartedly through prayer. James very clearly gave an explanation: "You want something but don't get it. You kill and covet, but you cannot have what you want. You quarrel and fight. You do not have, because you do not ask (pray to) God." (James 4: 2). Abraham Lincoln once said, "I have been driven many times to my knees by the overwhelming conviction that I had nowhere else to go. My own wisdom, and that of all about me, seemed insufficient for the day." King William prayed thus before he went to battle, "O God, if in the day of battle I forget Thee, do not Thou forget me."

There is nothing to hide when in supplication, we reach into the very depths of our lives and admit our needs and failures. In doing so, our hearts are quietened, our pride is stripped and we enjoy the presence of God. "Draw near to God and He will draw near to you." (James 4: 8)[2]

For a believer prayerlessness is sin. There is no easier sin to commit than the sin of prayerlessness. Samuel said to Israel, "As for me, far be it from me that I should sin against the LORD by failing to pray for you. And I will teach you the way that is good and right." (1 Samuel 12:23).

O. Hallesby has written, "A child of God cannot grieve Jesus in a worse way than to neglect prayer ... ."[3] Those who are careless about prayer show that they are careless about spiritual things. They are rarely ready to be used by God. Prayerlessness means unavailability to God - a sin against God's love. The person without prayer is more carnal than spiritual. "In the same way, the Spirit helps us in our weakness. We do not know what we ought to pray for, but the Spirit himself intercedes for us through wordless groans"

---

[2] *http://www.cann.org/prayer/pmyer.htm.* (24th Jan.).

[3] Hallesby, Prayer (London: Hodder & Stoughton, 1936), 48-49.

(Romans 8.26). He prompts us to pray, guides us in prayer, and helps us in our weakness in prayer. Christians without prayer are not filled and controlled by the spirit, no matter what they may profess.

NOTES

8

How Do You Motivate Yourself To Pray?

Can we motivate ourselves to pray? The answer is, "Yes," but there are few conditions. I am the person who chooses what I eat, and what I wear. I do not eat everything that comes to me, and I do not wear everything fashionable. This is because I have the freedom of choice in these matters. But, what if I fall ill, or am served food not to my liking, or am expected to wear clothes that don't suit me? Depending upon circumstances I sometimes have to compromise and have to do somethings simply because I have no choice. It is likewise in our relationship with God.

There are few conditions listed below:

Firstly, one has to be born in Christ's family

"Yet to all who did receive him, to those who believed in his name, he gave the right to become children of God—." (John 1: 12)

Secondly, one has to be passionate about talking to God

"During the days of Jesus' life on earth, he offered up prayers and petitions with fervent cries and tears to the one who could save him from death, and he was heard because of his reverent submission." (Hebrews 5: 7)

Lastly, one has to pray diligently

We have to be aware of whom we are talking to, and be sincere. "So what shall I do? I will pray with my spirit, but I will also pray with my understanding; I will sing with my spirit, but I will also sing with my understanding." (1 Corinthians 14: 15)

OUR SAVIOR IS THE EXAMPLE

Lord Jesus spent the whole night in prayer (Luke 6:12). Another time he woke up before dawn to pray (Mark 1: 35). After the miraculous feeding of several thousand people on the northern shores of Galilee, some who had witnessed the miracle wanted to make Jesus their king right on the spot. He responds by sending everyone away before going off by himself to pray (John 6:14,15; Mark 6:46). Evidently Jesus spent a considerable amount of time praying. Why? Since he was the Son of God he was not expected to pray.

These are the reasons:

1. To demonstrate his dependence on the Father

2. To introduce a new relationship between (intercession) us and the Father

3. To establish new goal for his disciples

The key to understanding prayer- life of Christ lies in the unique character of Jesus himself. Although He was fully God, the second member of the trinity, co-equal, co-eternal, and co-existent with

God the Father and the Holy Spirit, He was also fully human. The exceptional blend of natures in the person of Jesus of Nazareth is what theologians call the theanthropic nature of the Son of God. This unusual term derives from the combination of two Greek words: One meaning God-rheas-and the other meaning man-anthropos). Jesus was not only God and not only a man: he was a 'God-man' - fully God and yet fully human.

These are a few suggestions to motivate yourself towards prayer

1. Ask the Holy Spirit to give you His love, passion and zeal.

2. Bound assures us, "It is not in our power, perhaps to create fervency of Spirit at will, but we can pray to God to implant it. It is our responsibility, then, to nourish and cherish it, to guard it against extinction, to prevent its abatement or decline."[1]

3. Read the scripture portions of how God has called people to prayer and answered their prayers.

4. Discipline your prayer life without any compromises. God will really honor your prayers.

5. Take several major concerns of prayer and burden your heart to pray for the situation in the country, in your community and in your city. You can also get insights through news channels, newspaper, special prayer meetings or several other events.

6. Always be sensitive to the burden God gives you. Sometimes it is insignificant for others but it is very important for you to know that God wants you to be a channel of blessings through apparently insignificant things.

---

[1] E. M. Bounds, The Necessity of prayer (New York: Reveil, 1920), 59.

7.   Unite with those who are prayer minded people like you. It is very important that you have fellowship where you spend time with prayer warriors and that they help you to learn more maturity in prayer through each other's fellowship. God likes the unity of prayer-minded people.

In the words of E. M. Bounds: "Prayer must be red hot. The fervent prayer is effective ... It takes fire to make prayers go. Warmth of soul creates an atmosphere to make prayers go. Warmth of soul creates an atmosphere favorable to prayer ... By flame prayer ascends to heaven. Yet fire is not fuss, not heat, noise.... To be absorbed in God's will, to be so greatly in earnest about doing it that our whole being takes fire is the qualifying condition of the man who would engage in effectual prayer."[2]

Thought   :   The next time you feel reluctant to pray, ask yourself this question: "If Jesus relied on the Father through prayer, what makes me think, I don't need to?"

---

[2] *Ibid.,* 56.

NOTES

9

Hindrances To Prayer

Millions of Christians the world over lament that they do not receive answers to their prayers. Is it because the Most High fails to keep His promises? Or have we Christians, somewhere along the line, misunderstood the mandatory conditions that must be met before meaningful results can be obtained? Obviously the Almighty is not at fault in the matter of unanswered prayer. Why then are so many prayers not answered? The fact is, we must look within ourselves to track down the hindrances that so often rob us of the results we desperately seek. Some hindrances are:

1. UNCONFESSED SINS

The first is unconfessed sins. The most obvious hindrance to a prayerful life are the unconfessed sins in the heart of the one who is praying. Our God is holy, and our unconfessed sins create a barrier between Him and us when we come to Him. "But your iniquities have separated you from your God; your sins have hidden his face from you, so that he will not hear." (Isaiah 59:2). David concurred, knowing from experience that God is far from those who try to hide their sins: "If I had cherished sin in my heart, the Lord would not have listened;" (Psalms 66:18).

2. UNBELIEF AND DOUBT

A major hindrance to effective prayer is unbelief and doubt. Doubt is a form of unrighteousness, just as faith is a form of righteousness. Doubt is an action of the mind that disbelieves God; it is the silent mistrust of the Almighty's Word. Doubt is tantamount to calling the Most High a liar! Doubt is a sin of the mind, possibly one of the first sins ever committed. Praying without doubt means praying in the secure belief and understanding of God's character, nature, and motives. "And without faith it is impossible to please God, because anyone who comes to him must believe that he exists and that he rewards those who earnestly seek him." (Hebrews 11:6)

When we come to God in prayer, doubting His character, purpose, and promises, we insult Him terribly. Our confidence must be in His ability to grant any request that is in accordance with His will and purpose for our lives. We must pray with the understanding that whatever He purposes is the best. "But when you ask, you must believe and not doubt, because the one who doubts is like a wave of the sea, blown and tossed by the wind. That person should not expect to receive anything from the Lord." (James 1: 6,7)

Of course, doubt is a very human and common weakness. But doubting God and His word is deadly; and, a major obstacle to spiritual progress.

These quotations from the scriptures emphasise how much we should trust God in every way:

Matthew 21: 21,22   Jesus replied, "Truly I tell you, if you have faith and do not doubt, not only can you do what was done to the fig tree, but also you can say to this mountain, 'Go, throw yourself into the sea,' and it will be done. If you believe, you will receive whatever you ask for in prayer."

Mark 11:22-24   "Have faith in God," Jesus answered. "Truly I tell you, if anyone says to this mountain, 'Go, throw yourself into the sea,' and does not doubt in their heart but believes that what he says will happen, it will be done for him. Therefore I tell you, whatever you ask for in prayer, believe that you have received it, and it will be yours."

James 1: 6-8   But when you ask, you must believe and not doubt, because the one who doubts is like a wave of the sea, blown and tossed by the wind. That person should not expect to receive anything from the Lord. Such a person is double-minded and unstable in all he does.

Romans 14:23   … everything that does not come from faith is sin.

The answer to this problem is to go back to square one and sort out your own faith; because therein lies the problem and the solution.

3. SELFISH MOTIVES

Another hindrance to prayer is selfish motives. When our prayers are selfishly motivated, when we ask God for what we want rather than for what is His will, our motives hinder our prayers. "This is the confidence we have in approaching God: that if we ask anything according to his will, he hears us." (1 John 5: 14). Asking, according to God's will is the same as asking in submission, to whatever His will may be, whether or not we know what that will is. As in all things, Jesus is to be our example in prayer. "Father, if you are willing, take this cup from me; yet not my will, but yours be done." (Luke 22: 42). Selfish prayers are intended for the gratification of our own selfish desires, and we should not expect God to respond to such prayers. "When you ask, you do not receive, because you ask with wrong motives, that you may spend what you get on your pleasures." (James 4: 3)

Worthless objectives and selfish motives are another cause for unanswered prayer. Believers often ask for what appears - to them - be the right things, but they ask with the wrong motives. Believe it or not, it's quite possible to be totally ignorant of one's own motives - to actually think that you are asking with the right motive, and all the while to be totally wrong! We are all guilty of this error - including me.

God, however, looks upon the heart. He recognizes our motives and His answer is often 'no.' Therefore, if we are to be successful in prayer, we must diligently and constantly examine our motives. Failure to do so will result in fruitless prayers. Self deception is a common fault.

To be more successful always end a prayer request with these words:

"…not my will, but yours be done.." (Luke 22:42) Many Christians need to include the practice of ending a prayer with "your will be done." They need to be in touch with the Scriptures and the example set by the Savior Himself. (Matthew 26:42; Luke 22:42).

4. LACK OF FORGIVENESS TOWARDS OTHERS

In the book "Kneeling Christian" it is mentioned "Let this thought burn itself into your memory: the more like Christ Jesus a man becomes, the less he will judge other people. It is an infallible test. Those who are always criticizing others have drifted away from Christ. They may still be his, but they have lost His spirit of love. Beloved reader, if you have a criticizing nature, allow it to dissect yourself and never your neighbor."

A major hindrance to effective prayer is a spirit of unforgiveness toward others. When we refuse to forgive others, a root of bitterness grows in our hearts and chokes our prayers. How can we expect God to pour out His blessings upon us undeserving sinners if we harbour hatred and bitterness toward others? This principle is beautifully illustrated in the parable of the unforgiving servant in Matthew 18: 23-35. This story teaches that God has forgiven us - a debt that is beyond measure (our sin), and He expects us to forgive others as we have been forgiven. To refuse to do so will hinder our prayers.

These biblical references can encourage us:

Mark 11:25,26   "And when you stand praying, if you hold anything against anyone, forgive them, so that your Father in heaven may forgive you your sins."

Job 42:10   "After Job had prayed for his friends, the LORD restored his fortunes and gave him twice as much as he had before."

5. LAZINESS

There are certain things the Most High will never do for us humans. They are the things we can do for ourselves. He will not plough our fields, sow our crops nor weed our gardens. These are our duties, our responsibilities and if we do them faithfully. He will do His part. He will make things grow and produce the harvest. Thus working together with Him we will receive a bountiful blessing. But we must do our part - however small that part may be; because He will not do it for us.

Judges 6:14   "The LORD turned to him and said, "Go in the strength you have and save Israel out of Midian's hand. Am I not sending you?"

Note also King Hezekiah's efforts before he prayed for divine assistance. He didn't leave everything to God; he did what he could - with all his might.

2 Chronicles 31: 20,21 "This is what Hezekiah did throughout Judah, doing what was good and right and faithful before the LORD his God. In everything that he undertook in the service of God's temple and in obedience to the law and the commands, he sought his God and worked wholeheartedly. And so he prospered."

2 Chronicles 32: 5-8   "Then he worked hard repairing all the broken sections of the wall and building towers on it. He built another wall outside

that one and reinforced the supporting terraces of the City of David. He also made large numbers of weapons and shields. He appointed military officers over the people and assembled them before him in the square at the city gate and encouraged them with these words: "Be strong and courageous. Do not be afraid or discouraged because of the king of Assyria and the vast army with him, for there is a greater power with us than with him. With him is only the arm of flesh, but with us is the LORD our God to help us and to fight our battles." And the people gained confidence from what Hezekiah the king of Judah said.

Sometimes we become so lazy that we just expect God will do everything; and, being human, we do not have to do anything. But God plays His part, and expects us to play our part - with all sincerity.

6. UNUNITED PRAYER

Though secret prayer is a very good thing, there are occasions when we ought to call in the help of other believers. A joint request of two or more petitioners brings amazing results. Like a petition signed by many folk, or a rope of several strands, a group's prayers often carry more weight than would a solo prayer. Even the Master asked the disciples to watch and pray with him at his time of greatest need.

Matthew 18:19-20   "Again, truly I tell you that if two of you on earth agree about anything you ask for, it

will be done for you by my Father in heaven.
For where two or three gather in my name,
there am I with them."

7. INGRATITUDE

Ingratitude saddens the heart of the Most High. Indeed ingratitude
saddens the heart of anyone who has done something worthwhile
for another. We humans are unable to repay God for His amazing
sacrifice. But He is not looking for payment. In fact we couldn't
pay Him anyway - we're too poor. What the Almighty does expect
- and rightfully so - is gratitude, our thankfulness.

Failure to show gratitude when the Most High grants a request
will frustrate future prayers, reducing their prospect of success.

Ingratitude is a cruel blow to any giver. It kills future
generosity. In the spiritual realm ingratitude stifles prayer. It is a
major reason why many prayers go unanswered. Indeed ingratitude
is classified as one of the sins of the last days.

2 Timothy 3:1-5   "But mark this: There will be terrible times
                         in the last days. People will be lovers of
                         themselves, lovers of money, boastful,
                         proud, abusive, disobedient to their parents,
                         ungrateful,   unholy, without   love,
                         unforgiving, slanderous, without self-
                         control, brutal, not lovers of the good,
                         treacherous, rash, conceited, lovers of
                         pleasure rather than lovers of God— having
                         a form of godliness but denying its power.
                         Have nothing to do with such people."

1 Thessalonians 5:18   give thanks in all circumstances; for this is
                         God's will for you in Christ Jesus."

8. A HUSBAND WHOSE ATTITUDE TOWARD HIS WIFE IS LESS THAN GODLY

Finally, discord in the home is a definite obstacle to prayer. Peter specifically mentions this as a hindrance to the prayers of a husband whose attitude toward his wife is less than godly. "Husbands, in the same way be considerate as you live with your wives, and treat them with respect as the weaker partner and as heirs with you of the gracious gift of life, so that nothing will hinder your prayers." (1 Peter 3:7). Where there is serious conflict in family relationships and the head of the household does not demonstrate the attitudes Peter mentions, the husband's prayer and communication with God is hindered. Likewise, wives are to follow the biblical principles of submission to their husbands' headship if their own prayers are not to be hindered, "Wives, submit to your husbands as to the Lord. For the husband is the head of the wife as Christ is the head of the church, his body, of which he is the Saviour. Now as the church submits to Christ, so also wives should submit to their husbands in everything." (Ephesians 5:22-24)

Thought   -   Fortunately, all these hindrances to prayer can be dealt with at once by coming to God with prayers of confession and repentance. We are assured that "If we confess our sins, he is faithful and just and will forgive us our sins and purify us from all unrighteousness." (1 John 1: 9) Once we have done that, we can enjoy a clear and open channel of communication with God, and not only will our prayers be heard and answered, but we will also be filled with a deep sense of joy.

NOTES

10

How to Overcome Hindrances in Prayer?

There are some ways by which one can overcome hindrances to prayer but one has to be consistent.

THE BLOOD OF CHRIST

We have access to the throne of grace by a conscious acknowledgement of the power and the merits of the blood of Christ, for it gives us a strong footing against the enemy. "They triumphed over him

by the blood of the Lamb
and by the word of their testimony;
they did not love their lives so much
as to shrink from death." (Revelation 12:11)

PRAISE AND THANKS

Our prayers must be wrapped-up in praise and thanksgiving. "Yet you are enthroned as the Holy One; you are the praise of Israel." (Psalm 22: 3). When the presence of God becomes more and more real in our lives, we get absorbed in the spirit of prayer and distractions are more easily overcome. "Do not be anxious about anything, but in every situation, by prayer and petition, with thanksgiving, present your requests to God." (Philippians 4:6)

BE FOCUSED

When there is no focus in prayer, one's mind begins to wander. Be definite and specific about your requests. Keeping a prayer list and praying over the items one by one is very effective. Nowhere in the Bible do we find a command to close our eyes in prayer!

SELECT A PLACE

Oswald J. Smith used to walk up and down in his prayer closet with his eyes open and praying aloud. As far as possible one must choose a place where there is least disturbance and noise from the outside world. Jesus did teach us to shut the doors of our rooms before we begin to pray!

APPLY DIFFERENT WAYS TO SPEAK TO GOD

God is eager to listen to you. He did not set any system to talk to Him. He only needs to hear your voice. Prayer is a means of conversation with God. I have found that praying with an open Bible is extremely helpful. In this regard, we can pray and read the Bible. "In the first year of Darius son of Xerxes (a Mede by descent), who was made ruler over the Babylonian kingdom— in the first year of his reign, I, Daniel, understood from the Scriptures, according to the word of the LORD given to Jeremiah the prophet, that the desolation of Jerusalem would last seventy years. So I turned to the Lord God and pleaded with him in prayer and petition, in fasting, and in sackcloth and ashes." (Daniel 9.1-3) Daniel read the scriptures, and prayed . This is another way of praying to God.

Thought   :   We have to overcome the "I" (self-centeredness) factor to overcome hindrances to prayer.

NOTES

11

Who is a Prayer Partner and Why We Need One?

In many prayer books, this topic is not mentioned. A prayer partner is like a prayerful life partner. It is not a short-term relationship but a long-term one . The Bible says, "Again, I tell you that if two of you on earth agree about anything you ask for, it will be done for you by my Father in heaven." (Matthew 18: 19)

A PRAYER PARTNER IS SOMEONE:

* who spends rime in prayer and fasting with you

* who should have the right information about you and pray specifically for you

* who is mature - not only age-wise but also spiritually mature

* who can counsel one through the Word of God and with his/her experiences

* encourages you to grow in God and to have a child like faith

* who encourages one to grow in the fruit and gift of the spirit

*   who is God centered and not looking only at personal achievements

*   is someone whose own family testifies about him/ her

*   who views you in a balanced way

*   who is committed to share Christ with others

*   who is practical in the application of God's word in his/her own life

*   who is a model for others in his/her prayer life

*   who walks everyday with Christ Jesus

Many people are proud about their past experiences in the ministry or in their personal lives . But Jesus is always interested to know if you are with Him today. He is interested in your present status not the past . That is why Psalmist describes his relationship with Yahweh in Psalm 23.1, "The Lord is my shepherd" .... Here the word "is" has more importance than shepherd and Lord for he speaks of the continuity of his relationship with God.

WHY IS A PRAYER PARTNER IMPORTANT?

While two individuals can lift 100 pounds each, they can lift 300 pounds together. This is synergy! Charles Simpson once quoted a study that showed that two horses, working together pulling the same load, created so much horse power that it was as if a third horse had been added. This is synergy, too. Think about it. God established a law dictating that in the natural realm multiplied power would be released through agreement, harmony and unity.[1]

---

[1] Durch Sheets & William Ford III, History Makers (U.S.A: Regal Books, California, 2004), 52.

The psalmist proclaims, "How good and pleasant it is when brothers live together in unity!" (Psalm 133: 1) Do we really believe such harmony is possible, or is this a mere sentimental fantasy? The Apostle Paul said: "May the God who gives endurance and encouragement give you a spirit of unity among yourselves as you follow Christ Jesus, so that with one heart and one voice you may glorify the God and Father of our Lord Jesus Christ." (Romans 15. 5,6)

Harmony among brothers and sisters in a family of faith attracts the Father's favour.[2] These are some Bible verses which stress the importance of a prayer partner.

1. For strength:- "Though one may be overpowered, two can defend themselves. A cord of three strands is not quickly broken." (Ecclesiastes 4:12)

2. For encouragement:- "If one of them falls down, his friend can help him up. But pity the one who falls and has no one to help him up!" (Ecclesiastes 4: 10)

3. For success - "Two are better than one, because they have a good return for their labor:" (Ecclesiastes 4: 9)

4. For defense - "If one of them falls down, his friend can help him up. But pity the one who falls and has no one to help him up." (Ecclesiastes 4: 10)

5. For added faith - "Again, truly I tell you that if two of you on earth agree about anything you ask for, it will be done for you by my Father in heaven." (Matthew 18:19)

---

[2] Tom white, city- Wide Prayer Movements: One church and Many congregations (U.S.A: Servant publications,2001), p.42.

"For in the gospel a righteousness of God is revealed, a righteousness that is by faith from first to last, just as it is written: 'The righteous will live by faith'." (Romans 1: 17)

"And without faith it is impossible to please God, because anyone who comes to him must believe that he exists and that he rewards those who earnestly seek him." (Hebrews11: 6)

6.   To overcome our limitations: "The eye cannot say to the hand, 'I don't need you!' And the head cannot say to the feet, 'I don't need you!' (1 Corinthians 12: 21)

Prayer Partners need to:

1.   Reciprocate: Paul prayed for the Thessalonians, "We always thank God for all of you, mentioning you in our prayers." (1 Thessalonians 1: 2) Then he made a request: " Brothers and sisters, pray for us." (1 Thessalonians 5: 25)

2.   Be specific: Paul wanted to go and see the Romans, so he requested, " I urge you, brothers and sisters, by our Lord Jesus Christ and by the love of the Spirit, to join me in my struggle by praying to God for me. Pray that I may be kept safe from the unbelievers in Judea and that my service in Jerusalem may be acceptable to the Lord's people there, so that I may come to you with joy, by God's will, and in your company be refreshed." (Romans 15: 30- 32)

3.   Protect: Paul faced death and wrote to the people of Corinth, "Indeed, in our hearts we felt the sentence of death. But this happened that we might not rely on ourselves but on God, who raises the dead. He has delivered us from such a deadly peril, and he will deliver us again. On him we have set our hope that he will continue to deliver us, as you help us by your prayers. Then many will give thanks on our behalf for

the gracious favour granted us in answer to the prayers of many." (2 Corinthians 1: 9-11)

4. Deliverance: In prison Paul wrote : "for I know that though your prayers and the help given by of the Spirit of Jesus Christ what has happened to me will turn out for my deliverance." (Philippians 1: 19)

5. For preparation : Paul wanted Philemon to prepare a guest room for him - "And one thing more: Prepare a guest room for me, because I hope to be restored to you in answer to your prayers." (Philemon 1. 22)

Thought   :   Are you a prayer partner?

NOTES

12

A Prayer Chain

The Bible commands, "pray continually" (1 Thessalonians 5.17). A prayer chain is one of the methods of praying without ceasing. The enemy is constantly looking for opportunities to attack. The vital force that opposes him has to be on duty night and day. This is the force of intercessors. They stand in the gap without ceasing. They pleaded with the Lord without ceasing, as it is written in the Bible, in the battle with Amalek. The prayer chain ensures us by the reminder of the hands of the Moses that were permanently raised up, to guarantee victory to Israel.

A PRAYER CHAIN MUST ORIGINATE FROM GODAND BE DIRECTED TO A GOAL

The Lord said, " I have posted watchmen on your walls, Jerusalem;

they will never be silent day or night. You who call on the LORD,

give yourselves no rest, and give him no rest till he establishes Jerusalem

and makes her the praise of the earth." (Isaiah 62:6,7)

A Prayer chain is like a monitor that continually prays over the activities of the wicked one and all of his allies. They are to serve as security guards. God is the one who sets up watchmen. God must be the one who initiates each prayer chain.

God must give the vision of what he wants to do. That vision will be given to a person who seeks God's face and waits before him. The vision from the Lord will result in burden. The burden itself must be from the Lord. If not, it will be short-lived. What God does lasts. It cannot be over thrown. It cannot vanish like mist. The burden will grow until it becomes such that it cannot be executed. The person who is bearing it would feel like collapsing. When God puts the burden in a heart to have a prayer chain until the man becomes restless with it, the burden will give way to action, and that action is the establishment of a prayer chain. Therefore, there must be a vision that gives birth to a burden, and that results in action.

The goal is to be accomplished by the prayer chain and must be such that the people praying are compelled to pray, giving themselves fully to God. This means that those who are to be involved in praying, or a prayer chain must be men and women who will fight in this spiritual warfare. They must be people who must win or perish. Those who have decided that they must receive an answer from the Lord, having decided so, they put all their efforts into it night and day and pray without ceasing.

A PRAYER CHAIN CANNOT BE ESTABLISHED WITHOUT GOD

A prayer chain is established to deal with Satan. This makes it imperative for those involved in praying on a prayer chain to have experience in spiritual warfare. They will have to intercede to the Father for the work to be done, or the work being done, with a prayerful intercession against satanic powers. They will carry the instruments for building the kingdom of God on the one hand; and on the other hand, carry the weapons for the destruction of the work of Satan.

Nehemiah did this very thing. " Hear us, our God, for we are despised. Turn their insults back on their own heads. Give them over as plunder in a land of captivity. Do not cover up their guilt or blot out their sins from your sight, for they have thrown insults in the face of the builders.

So we rebuilt the wall till all of it reached half its height, for the people worked with all their heart. But when Sanballat, Tobiah, the Arabs, the Ammonites and the people of Ashdod heard that the repairs to Jerusalem's walls had gone ahead and that the gaps were being closed, they were very angry. They all plotted together to come and fight against Jerusalem and stir up trouble against it. But we prayed to our God and posted a guard day and night to meet this threat.

Meanwhile, the people in Judah said, "The strength of the labourers is giving out, and there is so much rubble that we cannot rebuild the wall." Also our enemies said, "Before they know it or see us, we will be right there among them and will kill them and put an end to the work."

Then the Jews who lived near them came and told us ten times over, "Wherever you turn, they will attack us." Therefore I stationed some of the people behind the lowest points of the wall at the exposed places, posting them by families; with their swords, spears and bows. After I looked things over, I stood up and said to the nobles, the officials and the rest of the people, "Don't be afraid of them. Remember the Lord, who is great and awesome, and fight for your brothers, your sons and your daughters, your wives and your homes."

When our enemies heard that we were aware of their plot and that God had frustrated it, we all returned to the wall, each to our own work. From that day on, half of my men did the work, while the other half were equipped with spears, shields, bows and armour. The officers posted themselves behind all the people of Judah who were building the wall. Those who carried materials did their work with one hand and held a weapon in the other, and each of the builders wore his sword at his side as he worked. But the man who sounded the trumpet stayed with me." (Nehemiah 4: 6-18)

When a prayer chain is established to accomplish a certain desire or work that is in the heart of God, that goal must be jealously guarded. If not, it will be stolen by the enemy. One of the chief tactics of the enemy is to confuse the vision. He may attempt to take it away completely, or he may add many other issues. When that happens, he has gained ground significantly. To avoid the enemy from wreaking havoc in this way, the goal of a prayer chain should be written on the wall of the room being used for the prayer chain. It will be possible to have the initial goal enlarged, but the goal will have to be maintained; and it will have to be precise.

Thought   :   A prayer chain can continue as long as the burden lasts; the vision and the burden must be protected by intense prayer. The heart must be kept steady and not open to every idea floating around in the name of a work for God. In fact every watchman must be merciful, but should also be narrow-minded.

NOTES

13

Prayer Walking

Prayer walking is moving your prayer closet or prayer meeting outside the four walls of a building. Often our prayers wobble between trivial matters of our own selfishness and topics of remote interest.

However, prayer walking focuses believers on real needs, the real hurts, and the real concerns of their community. As believers prayer walk, God gives them an awareness for people and their needs. It enables believers to intercede with power for people in their cities and communities.

A prayer walk is defined as, "praying on-site with insight." It is an active strategy that calls Christians to identify targeted places and then to physically move about those premises to cover them in prayer. It is praying in the places that you long for God to work. It is moving outside the four walls of the church and praying on city streets or roads for the people and places around you. When you go on the scene, different sights, smells, and sounds will prompt you to pray in ways that you would probably never think of if you were to pray from a remote location.

A prayer walk represents a person's or a group's active commitment to pray for a neighborhood, community, or any place that is on their mind. Often churches have chosen a specific time to gather for the purpose of corporately praying for areas of their city. Some may walk together around their church building requesting the Lord's blessings or guidance for their congregation or leadership.

The Bible tells us: "And pray in the Spirit on all occasions with all kinds of prayers and requests. With this in mind, be alert and always keep on praying for all the Lord's people." (Ephesians 6: 18): and, "pray continually" (1 Thessalonians 5:17). We can pray without formalities at any time – while walking, jogging or driving our car. But to pray with others can muster encouragement, strength, and a demonstration of a unity of faith.

That belief may come from the statement: "For where two or three gather in my name, there am I with them." (Mathew 18: 20). There are numerous Scriptures that address unity and prayer but none specifically instruct us to 'prayer walk'; neither are there scriptures that say we should not do so.

How to Prayer Walk - The Origins

The original idea for a 'prayer walk' may have come from the account in Joshua Chapter 6, where God directed the Israelites to march around the city of Jericho. After the designated number of rounds of the city the people were told to shout loudly when the priests blew their trumpets. Their obedience brought down the walls of the city. However, a prayer walk does not have to include those two particular elements also.

Regardless of the specific purpose in your prayer walk, you can know that the Lord does hear and honour your request. He can change a neighborhood, community, and whole nations with unified prayer. As importantly, God can change individual hearts and lives. That is the beginning of changing everything else. If you want to pray for your declining neighborhood, for your town's red light district, or for your own life to be changed by the power of God, pray and ask the Lord to honour your petitions.

On your prayer walk, you might keep this verse in mind, "This is the confidence we have in approaching God: that if we ask anything according to his will, he hears us. And if we know that he hears us—whatever we ask—we know that we have what we asked of him." (1 John 5:14, 15)

THREE IMPORTANT FACTORS FOR A PRAYER WALK

The first important factor for a prayer walk is Intercession. It means an intercession for people and their needs. While you walk, you call on God to work in and bless the people of a street, a road, a community, or a city. It is the deliberate activity of interceding for others as one walks by their homes or businesses. In a prayer walk, a believer focuses on people and their cities or communities with a specific plan of intercession. The believer calls on God to bless, to save, to change, and to use the people who live in the houses or work in the businesses.

The second important factor for prayer walk is on-site prayer. It is simply praying in the very places where you expect your prayers to be answered. It is praying in the places where you long to see God work. One can pray as he or she walks by a building or house. There can be exceptions to this. One can routinely break from walking to take a deliberate stance at special spots or station oneself at elevated viewpoints. This is for the purpose of intentionally praying for a place and the people who are there. Whether walking or stationed at a place, you are praying at the place where you desire and long for God to work and to pour out His abundant blessings. It is going to the place and praying where you hunger for God to send His power and His blessings.

Finally, a prayer walk is praying on-site with insight. You can receive this insight in a variety of ways.

One way is responsive insight. This is the insight that you receive as you look at, and observe, the people and the surroundings. When people prayer walk, they do it with their eyes wide open. By seeing the people, their homes, and their businesses, it floods their prayers with significance. The ordinary powers of observation yield tremendous insights about the best focus in prayer. These insights will refine their prayers and will give a more powerful and sharper focus to their prayers. By having this more powerful and sharper focus in prayer, it will lead to a more fervent and ardent intercession.

The insight of the prayer walk may be researched insight. Before going on a prayer walk, believers can do research about their community or city. They can therefore understand the problems of the area and the hindrances to the gospel in this area. By doing this, they can develop a prayer strategy that will address these problems and these hindrances. This will allow them the opportunity to pray for solutions and for the removal of any obstacle to the spread of the gospel of Jesus Christ. Insight on how to pray can be given to the prayer walker as he or she prays through the Scripture.

Another way that one receives insight during a prayer walk is revealed insight. The Holy Spirit will reveal specific needs and concerns to pray over during the prayer walk. Because of this, it is crucial that the prayer walker pray the Scripture as he or she walks. This is due to the person, and the work of the Holy Spirit.

It is the Holy Spirit who reveals the truth of the Scripture, and who enables the believer to pray. As a believer prays the Scripture, the Holy Spirit will grant specific guidance in how to pray for individuals and cities or communities. As a believer saturates his life and prayers with the Word of God, the Holy Spirit can and does grant specific promptings to pray for a city or community and its individuals. Praying the Word of God opens your ears to listen to the prayer guidance of the Holy Spirit. The will enable the prayer walker to pray more specifically and more intensely.

The insights gained through a prayer walk can lead to powerful intercession for a city or a community and its people. These insights will enable the believer to seek God to deal with the problems and the barriers to the gospel so that God can be glorified by the advancement of His kingdom and the transformation of lives in cities and communities. These insights blend together to fortify prayer with a starkly relevant authenticity. It is no longer prayer as usual. This up-close and personal prayer becomes an adventure for humanity.

Thought   :   A prayer walk is not an occasionally beamed bundle of religious sentimentality toward people. It is directed and focused intercession. This is the strength of prayer walk. It is quality intercession for people. The best praying is always done on purpose and not as a casual coincidence. Quality prayer walk is not incidental; it is intentional!

NOTES

14

Theological Understanding of Prayer, Petition and Intercession

The three principles to understand the theology of prayer:

FIRST PRINCIPLE

God is present and active in, and within, all things. He is at the innermost heart of all reality, powerfully accomplishing His purposes. He is not present as a force alongside other forces, but as the Alpha, the ground and origin of the continuing reality of everything in the world;, and as the Omega, the attractive, drawing all things from within into the future- continually building up the universe in a process of evolution and development which affects the without from within, and continually drawing our minds and will to His love, and thus building up the community of the human race in Christ and in the Spirit.

1) God's power is not a dominating external force, but an all-embracing, unifying, up building, internal, energizing source and attractive goal. His power does not interfere with or interrupt the interplay of external forces, but He uses and guides them, much as the human will uses and guides some of the forces within the human body. Prayer is the means by which we bring our will into accord with the changeless will of God.

2) Does anything ever happen that wouldn't have happened if we had not prayed? If we genuinely pray, we authentically manifest a personal relationship with God in faith. Then our prayers as effective symbols enter into the order and instrumentally by which the whole of created reality is made present to God's giving and creative love. The world is being continually sustained and enriched as this love reaches it through the many complex interrelationships of actions, causes and effective symbols. Authentic prayer is one of these symbols effectively relating the world to the enriching power of God.

SECOND PRINCIPLE

Whatever we utter to God, either in the form of petitions or praises, may be authentically a manifestation of faith and trust, and a desire for deepening our relationship with God. It is not, of course, necessary that this always provides the immediate and direct motivation; but behind our petition, presented implicitly and truly, is the act of our complete dependence in God. Prayer and petition are nearly synonymous; God is addressed out of the depth of human weakness and need. God's people had other needs besides deliverance. These, too, are reflected in the prayers of the old covenant. They needed God's guidance and provision in the wilderness. The pillar of cloud and pillar of fire by which God lead the Israelites : to the manna and water from the rock to sustain them.[1]

FINAL PRINCIPLE

This principle which has not been addressed explicitly up until now, is the dialogical nature of divine providence. This is a conception of God's way of acting in the world as involving basically three moments: divine initiative, human response, and divine response to human response. The prayer intercedes on behalf of the subject, believing that God will answer the prayer accordingly.[2] This conception provides the background for the understanding of the intercession that is being proposed here. This conception of God's action in the world, of interacting with the world, appears in the earliest traditions of the Bible that we can discover (the document of the Pentateuch): and is constant from then on. We may briefly describe it in this way: God out of pure liberality, in an act of absolute gracious initiative, seeks to enrich us, by drawing us out of nothingness, our littleness, poverty, self centeredness and isolation: into a life of communion - sharing with him and with one another. This is divine grace.

The prayer of intercession is special in a way; for this prayer symbolizes our solidarity and our togetherness before God. What is given to each of us is to be shared by all of us as far as this is possible. If our relationship with others is one of openness; of caring and unselfish love; then our prayer of intercession effectively expresses the order of dependence, and communication, that God intends in the world. But if our relationship with others is a matter

---

[1] *http://www.beginningwithmoses.org/ articles/beprayers.pdf*

[2] *http://www.answers.com/topic/intercession*

of narrow, provincial concern; excluding some persons and finding pleasure in their failure, then our prayer of intercession does not express a desire for the coming of kingdom of God, and it is not answered.

NOTES

Bibliography

Lee, P.K.D. Add to YOUT Faith. Excellence. India: Haggai Institute, 2000.

Murray, Andrew. Ministry of Intercession. New York: Revell, 1898.

Anonymous, The Kneeling Christian.

Wagner Peter, C. Praying With Power. C.A. Light Publications, Ventura, 1997.

D.M. Melntyre, The Hidden Life of Prayer, 3rd ed. (London: Marshall, Morgan& Scott, n.d.), 87

Bryant, David. With Concerts of Prayer. CA Ventura, Calif Regal, 1954.

Bosech, Donald G. The Struggle of Prayer. San Francisco: Harper, 1980.

Wiley, Deborah: Ears to Hear. India: Ywam Publishing, Chennai, 1982.

Huegel, FJ. Successful Praying. Minneapolis: Bethany, 1959.

Sanders, Oswald. Praying Power Unlimited. Minneapolis: Billy Graham Evangelistic Association, 1977.

Wesley, John. Causes of Inefficiancy of Christianity," Sermons on Several Occasions, Ed. Thomas Jackson, 2 Vols. New York: T. Mason and G.Lane,1840.

Duewel, Wesley L. Mighty Prevailing Power: U:S.A: Zondervan Publishing House, 1990.

Hallesby, O. Prayer. London: Hodder & Stoughton, 1936.

East, Carolyn. Prayers That Avail Much. New Delhi: National Prayer Forum, 2003.

Gordan, S.D. Quiet Talks on Prayer. New York: Revell, 1904.

Heitz, Skip. When God Prays. Illinois: Tyndale House Publisher, Inc. Wheaton, 2003.

Forum, Zacharias Tanee. Moving God Through Prayer. New York: Vantage Press, 1989.

Forum, Zacharias Tanee. The Practice of Intercession. New York: Vantage Press, 1991.

Sheets, Dutch & Ford III, William. History Makers. U.S.A: Regal Press, California, 2004.

Duewel, Wesley L. Touch the World Through Prayer. U.SA: Grand Rapids, Zondervan Publishing House, 1986.

White, Tom. City wide Prayer Movements: One Church Many Congregations. U.S.A: Servant Publications, 2001.

http://mzbworks.home.att.net/prayer.htm

http://www.allaboutfollowingjesuS.org/sPiritual-warfare.htm

http://www.gitlingingrace.org/prayer/whyPray.html

http:// www.givingingrace.org/prayer/tvhyPray.html

http://www.orgs.ttu.edu/ivcf/prayer/why.asp

http://www.spirithome.com/unseen.html>

http://www.sw.mins.org/stratl.htm!>

http://www.sw.mins.org/stratI.html>

http:/thinkexist.com/quotes/with/keyword/prayers

http:/beginningwithmoses.org/articles/btprayer.pdf

http:/www.answer.com/topic/intercession

http://hannahscupboard.com/prayer-quotes.

http://www.goodreads.com/quotes/tag/prayer